THE $50 Dinner Party

26 Dinner Parties That Won't Break Your Bank, Your Back or Your Schedule

SALLY SAMPSON

A FIRESIDE BOOK
PUBLISHED BY SIMON & SCHUSTER

FIRESIDE
Rockefeller Center
1230 Avenue of the Americas
New York, NY 10020

FIRESIDE and colophon are registered trademarks
of Simon & Schuster Inc.
DESIGNED & ILLUSTRATED BY JILL WEBER

Manufactured in the United States of America

1 3 5 7 9 10 8 6 4 2

Library of Congress Cataloging-in-Publication Data
Sampson, Sally, 1955–
The $50 dinner party : 26 dinner parties that won't break your
bank, your back, or your schedule / Sally Sampson.
p.   cm.
"A Fireside book."
Includes index.
1. Dinners and dining.   2. Entertaining.   3. Menus.   I. Title.
TX737.S284   1998
642'.4—dc21   98-28265
                                                              CIP

ISBN 0-684-84228-9

For MARK,
WHO MAKES EVERY MEAL A DINNER PARTY
AND EVERY DINNER PARTY A TREAT TO GIVE.

And to LAUREN and BEN,
MY EXPERIMENTAL, VORACIOUS AND GRACIOUS CHILDREN,
WHO THINK THAT IT'S PERFECTLY NORMAL
TO HAVE FRIENDS OVER ALL THE TIME AND
ARE WILLING TO TRY JUST ABOUT ANYTHING I MAKE.

Acknowledgments

Thanks, as always, to my pals: dedicated, critical, analytical, enthusiastic and appreciative eaters.

Special thanks to my wonderful editor, Sydny Miner; my agent, Carla Glasser, without whom this book would never have happened; Colleen Graham, for testing recipes and loving my children, Benjamin and Lauren, while I sat at the computer; Nancy Olin, for her cheerful menu advice; and Todd English, for friendship, inspiration and having the very best restaurant in the world.

Contents

INTRODUCTION   13

A NOTE ABOUT MONEY   17

A NOTE ABOUT TIME   19

THE $50 PANTRY   21

THE $50 ARSENAL   27

BRUSCHETTA AND DIPS   31

MENU ONE   49
>   Moroccan Chicken, Fresh Herb Couscous, Red Onion and
>   Blood Orange Salad, Chocolate Date Nut Bars

MENU TWO   57
>   Caribbean Spiced Chicken, Coconut Black Bean Risotto, Cucumber Salad
>   with Yogurt and Mint, Key Lime Mousse with Toasted Coconut

MENU THREE   65
>   Rosemary Oregano Lamb Burgers, Roast Potatoes with Feta Cheese,
>   Romaine with Cucumbers and Tomatoes, Fresh Fruit with Berry Puree

MENU FOUR   71
>   Curried Swordfish with Cilantro Paste, Oven-Baked Corn, Sautéed
>   Cherry Tomatoes, Strawberry Rhubarb Compote

MENU FIVE   77
>   Classic Lasagna, Roasted Garlic Bread, Salad of Arugula, Endive
>   and Radicchio, Cookie Platter, Grapes and Melon

MENU SIX   85
Garlic Roasted Chicken with Pan-Roasted Vegetables, Orzo and
Broccoli Rabe, Chocolate Bread Pudding Drizzled with Heavy Cream

MENU SEVEN   91
Saffron Risotto with Pan-Broiled Fennel Shrimp, Pan-Broiled Zucchini,
Bibb Lettuce with Red Onion and Balsamic Vinaigrette, Italian Bread, Fresh
Raspberry Tart with Lemon Curd

MENU EIGHT   99
Chicken Curry with Coconut, Basil and Mangoes, Basmati Rice with
Toasted Pistachio Nuts, Steamed Green Beans, Roti, Nan or Chapati,
Vanilla Ice Cream with Bananas and Caramel Sauce

MENU NINE   105
Beef Carbonnade, Parsnip Mashed Potatoes, French Bread, Brussels
Sprouts Leaves with Brown Butter, Dain's Grandmother's Carrot Cake

MENU TEN   113
Roasted Chicken Breasts with Dried Figs, Apricots and Prunes,
French Bread, Mixed Green Salad with Red Onions and
Toasted Pine Nuts, Rice Pudding

MENU ELEVEN   119
Fresh Asparagus Salad, French Bread, Wild Mushroom Risotto with
Radicchio Salad, Pecan Butter Cookies and Fresh Berries

MENU TWELVE   123
Avgolemono Soup, Eggplant and Lamb Moussaka, Mixed Greens with
Pistachio-Lemon Dressing, Fresh Figs, Red Grapes and Pecan Butter
Cookies

Contents

MENU THIRTEEN   131

Chicken Saltimbocca with Panfried Sage Leaves, Roasted Butternut Squash
and Granny Smith Apples with Walnuts and Currants, Romaine
Salad with Anchovy Dressing, Trio of Sorbets and Cookie Platter

MENU FOURTEEN   137

Cashew Noodles with Asparagus and Peppers, Glazed Baby Back Ribs,
Asian Slaw, Ginger Ice Cream with Bittersweet Chocolate Sauce

MENU FIFTEEN   145

Prosciutto–Wrapped Mango Slices, Pasta Alfredo with Broccoli Rabe,
Crusty Italian Bread, Hazelnut Torte with Chocolate Glaze

MENU SIXTEEN   151

Chilled Corn Soup with Tomatoes, Red Peppers and Cilantro, Spice-
Rubbed Catfish, Polenta Triangles, Grilled Pineapple and Avocado Salad
with Walnut Oil Vinaigrette, Jake and Earl's Six–Layer Bars with
Chocolate, Pecans and Coconut

MENU SEVENTEEN   159

Three–Bean Chili with Tons of Garnishes, Corn Bread, Chips and Salsa,
Green Salad with Creamy Orange Dressing, Chewy Maple Cookies
and Vanilla Ice Cream

MENU EIGHTEEN   165

Grilled Marinated Flank Steak with Soy, Sherry and Dijon, Potato Cake
with Garlic and Olive Oil, Salad of Arugula, Avocado and Mango,
Cheesecake with Raspberry Sauce

MENU NINETEEN   173

Grilled Salmon Steaks with Citrus and Thyme, Pan–Steamed Spinach,
Leek Mashed Potatoes, Engagement Brownies

MENU TWENTY   179
Spicy Mustard Steak Tips, Mashed Sweet Potatoes, Seared Greens,
Chocolate Mousse Torte

MENU TWENTY-ONE   185
Bouillabaisse with Rouille, French Bread, Romaine Salad with Arugula,
Roquefort Cheese and Pears, Vanilla Ice Cream with Bittersweet
Chocolate Sauce and Raspberries

MENU TWENTY-TWO   191
Tuna au Poivre, Roasted Ratatouille, Roasted New Potatoes, French Bread,
Nectarine, Strawberry and Blueberry Crunch

MENU TWENTY-THREE   197
Chicken Fricassee, Egg Noodles or Rice, Steamed Fresh Peas,
Apple Crisp

MENU TWENTY-FOUR   201
Chilled Summer Minestrone, Italian Bread, Grilled Shrimp Skewers,
Lemon-Glazed Pecan and Coconut Squares

MENU TWENTY-FIVE   207
Spicy Scallops with Cashews, Steamed Basmati Rice, Watercress Salad
with Orange Segments, Vanilla Ice Cream with Roasted Peaches
and Gingerroot

MENU TWENTY-SIX   213
Ana Sortun's Brine-Cured Grilled Pork Loin with Spanish Tomato Salsa,
Steamed Rice, Grilled Asparagus, Crème Brûlée

Contents

$50 COOKIES   219
INDEX   229

Introduction

The idea for this book came from my friend and agent, Carla Glasser. She called me one day and said, "Sally, I have a book idea that's perfect for you: The $50 dinner party. What do you think?" Dinner parties for six, she explained, each costing no more than $50 (not including wine, coffee or tea). I loved the idea; I could picture the book exactly and the thought of having dinner parties and testing menus was wonderfully compelling.

Although I relished the idea, I wasn't sure I was the best person to write this book. From 1980 to 1989 I owned and ran From the Night Kitchen, a gourmet take-out shop in Brookline, Massachusetts. When I sold it I wasn't quite sure what I wanted to do, but I knew with certainty that I didn't want to spend a lot of time cooking. I also knew that I wanted to work at home. Right before I sold the shop, I wrote a cookbook, *Recipes from the Night Kitchen*, inspired by the soups I cooked, and discovered that I preferred writing about food to preparing it. In those days I never, ever cooked at home, so when I sold the shop, I got rid of almost every appliance and utensil I owned. I wanted to trade in my pots and pans for pen and paper, get rid of my Cuisinart and order a computer. However, I was cautioned not to quit my day job.

I didn't take the naysayer's advice; instead, I listened to my husband, Mark, who said, "Just write." I stopped cooking professionally and started writing. At first I wrote articles on different food-related subjects: "How to Eat Low Fat at High End Restaurants"; "Where to Eat in Boston for $20, $40, $60, $80 and $100"; and "What to cook for Idiot Proof Entertaining." I interviewed chefs about their secret eating habits, took them to convenience stores to see if they could make me a reasonable meal from their purchases and chronicled the opening of several now-successful restaurants. It was a lot of fun: I ate in great restaurants, met a lot of interesting and talented people, worked at home and cooked only for the pure pleasure of it.

Eventually, I wanted to write another cookbook and began cooking at home again, still for pleasure but now also for work: the recipes had to be tested. I wrote some more cookbooks and a lot of articles on food and eventually, whenever I cooked, I had a pencil nearby. The truth is my day job is writing about food and as it turns out, my night job is cooking the food I write about.

It never occurred to me that I would spend my days at home cooking, living in a house with a kitchen that had a wide assortment of appliances and tools of the trade, including: two Cuisinarts; a cappuccino machine; an ice cream maker; assorted copper, cast-iron, All Clad and Calphalon skillets too numerous to count; stockpots in every size; juicers; mixers; knives for slicing, paring, butchering, boning, chopping and skinning; a freezer filled with homemade stocks and broths (including veal, lobster and chicken); and a pantry overflowing with serving dishes, cookbooks, condiments and spices. I never dreamed that outside my kitchen door would sit a huge New Braunfels grill and smoker that my friend Verdi refers to as the Cannonball Express. I have not and never will succumb to buying a microwave or a lot of useless gadgets, like strawberry hullers and pastry crimpers, although I do have to admit that I own a mushroom-shaped wooden thing that squishes garlic cloves (it was a gift).

I work hard and have learned to be efficient with time, but I spend a lot of work time not working. Sometimes, as my fingers hit the computer keyboard, I am suddenly inspired to fold the laundry, make chicken stock, artfully arrange my children's toys, pay bills or worse yet, clean out the basement. Last week, I pulled weeds for over an hour, which says volumes about the condition of my garden, but that's another story (although I have discovered that one of the secrets to effortless meals is to have an herb garden).

Although my kitchen is an imperfect one, I love that I can move with such ease from computer to Cuisinart. I test every recipe I write about, whether it's my own or someone else's and fortunately, the best way to maximize my time is to have dinner parties. I need the feedback. But, the meals are based on what I need to test rather than on what makes sense to pair together. I don't give normal dinner parties: I might have six people over and serve only scallop dishes, or have four people over and serve two entire meals for six, from appetizer to dessert.

We've had so many dinner parties that my friends have become good friends with each other, bonding over being over fed and the thrill of being able to boldly critique my cooking. So dinner parties often consist of lively conversations about what goes well with what, whether something is too time consuming and whether or not one would actually be willing to do the work involved to make it, as opposed to just eating it.

Friends often comment on how calm I always seem during these gatherings. I've realized that dinner parties aren't as stressful for me as they are for others. As a rule, I do not invite anyone I'm trying to impress, so if something doesn't turn out just right or someone doesn't like something, it's okay: my ego is not on the line. Both the food and the guests tend to be eclectic; I don't worry about whether things go together. And until I began this book, I never served appetizers (more about that later). Almost every party is a buffet and almost everyone brings wine.

Surprisingly to most of our guests, our kitchen, although colorful and well equipped, is not particularly well designed. Although I dream of the next kitchen (an eat-in kitchen with floor-to-ceiling windows, a brick fireplace and big enough to house my children, my computer, my equipment, my cookbooks and whatever new kitchen exotica I desperately need), it seems to me that the best–designed, best–equipped kitchens are for people who don't actually cook.

So back to the $50 dinner party. It turns out that putting people and food together *is* a real challenge and that in the past I didn't really have to do it so I didn't have the experience to write this book. Now that I have, I understand why people get so tense: Will my guests like each other? Will they arrive in time for my oven schedule? Can I clean my house in time? Will I stain my new blouse? Will my children go to bed without trouble? Will the side dishes go with the entrée and will they have any room for dessert?

The answer is that most of it doesn't matter. You should cook because you love to and entertain because you want to be with your friends. After all, who are you trying to impress?

A Note About Money

I live outside Boston where it is no problem finding almost any ingredient. All the menus in this book cost me less than $50 to prepare, not including wine, coffee or tea. I bought ingredients in season and I had a well-stocked pantry, refrigerator and freezer, which means that if a dish called for any item I consider an essential ingredient (see page 21), I did not include it in the overall cost. Although I shopped at local grocery and specialty stores, in an effort to be conservative, I tried to base the cost on the most expensive price around. I bought only what I needed. If you live where specialty items are hard to find and you need to mail order (see page 21) ingredients, or if you buy ingredients out of season, you may spend more.

A NOTE ABOUT TIME

These menus were not created with the goal of saving time, but the reality of my life, like the reality of most people, required that they be economical in terms of time as well as money. I have two children who think that hanging out with me in the kitchen is a blissful thing, and I work at home, which means interruptions are routine. My point is that you should not be intimidated by any of the recipes in these pages because they were created with the demands and constraints of real life in mind.

THE $50 PANTRY

One of the most important things that anyone can do to make entertaining effortless is to have a well-stocked pantry, refrigerator and freezer. The following list may seem daunting but you may already have most of these items on your shelves. A painless way to build your pantry is to add an item or two to your basket each time you shop. Items like canned tomatoes, canned beans, mustards, vinegars and flours will last for a long time, while other ingredients have a more limited shelf life.

Dried Herbs and Spices

The quality of the herbs and spices you use can make or break a dish; buy the best you can afford. My favorite mail-order source is Penzey's in Wisconsin, 414/574-0277. Buy small amounts from a reputable spice company and use them within a year.

Basil

Bay leaves

Caraway seeds

Cardamom

Cayenne pepper

Chili powder

Cinnamon, ground

Cumin, ground

Curry powder

Fennel seeds

Ginger, ground

Marjoram

Nutmeg, ground

Oregano, Greek

Paprika, Hungarian sweet

Pepper: crushed red pepper flakes, black, white

Rosemary

Tarragon

Thyme

Pantry

The following list may look daunting, but with these ingredients on hand, cooking dinner will rarely involve more than a quick trip for items like produce, meat or dairy products. However, there are recipes that call for ingredients that I would not call essential, so on occasion you may have to buy a pantry item such as key lime juice, canned truffle peelings, pomegranate molasses or buttermilk.

CANNED FOODS

Beans, canned: chickpeas, dark red kidney, white
cannelini, black turtle

Chicken broth

Tomatoes: whole plum, chopped, paste

Vegetable broth

CONDIMENTS, OILS AND VINEGARS

Balsamic vinegar

Canola oil

Extra virgin olive oil

Mustard: Dijon, whole grain

Olive oil

Red wine vinegar

Soy sauce, light and dark

White wine vinegar

Wines, white and red (do not use cooking wine, which
has added salt; use only wines you would drink)

PASTA, RICE AND CRACKERS

Breadsticks

Chutney, assorted

Crackers, assorted

Pasta, dried, various shapes and sizes

Rice: white, arborio, basmati

The
$50
Pantry

BAKING

Baking powder

Baking soda

Chocolate, unsweetened and semisweet

Chocolate chips, semisweet

Cocoa powder, unsweetened, such as Droste or Callebaut

Flour: unbleached, all-purpose

Molasses, unsulfured, and pomegranate (available in
Middle Eastern specialty food shops)

Oats, old fashioned rolled

Sugar, white and brown

Vanilla extract

REFRIGERATOR

Anchovies packed in oil

Capers in brine

Cheese: Fresh Romano and Parmesan, in chunks (don't
bother with pregrated)

Olives, assorted black and green (the real kind you buy
in bulk in plastic containers, not canned)

FRUITS AND VEGETABLES

Apples, Granny Smith (the best overall apple, great for
eating and cooking)

Carrots

Celery

Garlic

Gingerroot

Lemons

Limes
Potatoes
Red onions
Shallots
Spanish onions

FREEZER

Cut-up chicken
French or Italian baguettes
Pecans
Unsalted butter
Vanilla ice cream
Walnuts

The
$50
Pantry

THE $50 ARSENAL

If you've ever visited the home or the restaurant of a professional chef, you may have noticed that they don't have tons of machines or big, fancy, expensive equipment. Those "tools" actually make easy tasks more complicated and time consuming (not to mention clogging up your kitchen drawers). Instead, professional chefs have what they consider truly essential equipment and in fact often make do with less, making one piece of equipment work for more uses than it was intended.

Keep in mind that expensive is not always better. Think about how much use something will get. For instance, if you sauté a lot, it makes sense to spend more money on a really good pan that can take a lot of abuse over a long period of time. On the other hand, if you rarely bake, don't buy anything more expensive than tempered glass or aluminum pans.

The following list includes some items that I consider absolutely necessary to have in a kitchen, no matter what you do, and some items that are necessary only for particular kinds of cooking. I've named my favorite brands if I think it makes a difference.

Assorted glass or ceramic mixing bowls

Assorted ladles: 4-ounce, 6-ounce

Assorted rubber spatulas

Assorted stainless steel mixing bowls

Assorted wooden spoons

Blender (Oster, a throwback to my childhood and my favorite blender)

Food processor (I am wedded to my Cuisinart)

Good resilient cutting board, wood or acrylic

Grill or hibachi

Kitchen timer

Long-handled, heavy-duty tongs for grilling

Measuring cups, heavy-gauge stainless steel

Measuring spoons, heavy-gauge stainless steel

Metal flue (chimney) for grilling: a cylinder made of sheet metal that you fill with newspaper and then top with charcoal. It heats up faster than placing the charcoal directly in the pit.

Pepper grinder (Perfex is my favorite)

Potholders; dish towels

Salad spinner

Slotted spoon

Stainless steel colander

Whisk

GADGETS

Can opener (Xyliss is expensive but worth every penny because it makes you want to find cans to open)

Cheese grater, stainless steel (I love Xyliss)

Citrus peeler

Garlic press (Susi is great)

Lemon zester

Meat thermometer (I recommend a tiny instant thermometer called Bitherm from Taylor)

Oven thermometer

Stainless steel skewers

Vegetable peeler (Westmark peeler makes it a joy to peel; I buy two at a time)

Wooden citrus juicer

POTS AND PANS

1 shallow roasting pan, 15 x 10 x 2-inch nonstick

2-quart saucepan

3-quart saucepan

8-inch skillet or sauté pan, nonstick

8-quart stockpot (I use Calphalon or All Clad)

9-inch cast-iron skillet (garage sales are good for these)

10-inch skillet or sauté pan, nonstick

Deep roasting pan with rack, 16 x 11 x 5-inch

KNIVES

4-inch paring knives

6-inch cook's knife

8-inch chef's knife

8-inch serrated bread knife

10-inch carving knife

Knife rack

Knife sharpening steel

Poultry shears

THE $50 ARSENAL

Wusthof/Dreizack makes heavy-duty knives of hand-forged high-carbon steel, suitable for commercial use, in just about every size and shape. Sabatier and Henckels are also good.

BAKING EQUIPMENT

8-INCH SQUARE PAN

9 X 12-INCH PAN

BAKING SHEET WITHOUT SIDES, 18 X 12 X 1-INCH

BUNDT PAN

Metal, glass or clay are all fine. If you're serious about baking and want to invest some money, try Kaiser La Forme, which is available at Williams-Sonoma. You'll probably never need to replace it: it's nonstick, double coated with silicone, and has a 5-year guarantee.

BRUSCHETTA AND DIPS

Although I am a big fan of starter courses at restaurants, I never make them at home. Long before I wrote cookbooks, I was a caterer, and after too many long nights stuffing pea pods, tomatoes and endive leaves for too little money, I realized that not only did I hate to make "pick-up" food, I didn't feel that the end result was worth the time involved. In addition, instead of teasing my appetite, I often felt that an hour of "little bites" satisfied it completely. Now I serve a few dips, some marinated olives, or set out a few very special cheeses and let guests pick and choose as they please.

The following recipes can all be made ahead in a short amount of time and with very little effort. Serve them with toasted bread, breadsticks, crudités and crackers. If you are really rushed for time, almost all have versions that are readily available at a well-stocked supermarket, or in specialty and ethnic food stores.

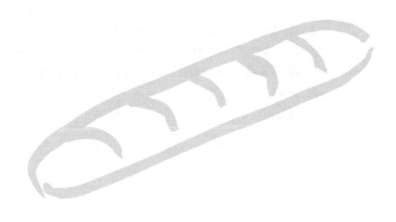

Bruschetta

I'm not going to give complete recipes here, but rather ideas for what to put on toasted or grilled bread. Traditionally, bruschetta is bread that has been grilled over a fire, rubbed with fresh garlic cloves, drizzled with extra virgin olive oil and sprinkled with kosher salt. If you don't have a fire, feel free to do the same in the toaster or oven or grill. When laziness overcomes me, I omit the garlic or use garlic oil instead of olive. It is great served alone or with any of the following toppings.

- OLIVE PUREE: Throw some chopped black or green olives in a food processor with a little olive oil and, if you want to get fancy, some anchovy fillets. Or you can purchase it at a grocery store. Serve with or without mozzarella cheese.
- Chopped fresh tomatoes, basil, a drizzle of olive oil and a few shavings of Parmesan cheese
- White bean puree topped with arugula leaves
- Roasted red peppers and anchovy fillets
- Melted mozzarella cheese, slices of roma tomatoes and basil leaves
- Cheddar cheese and salsa (completely untraditional but great served before an entrée like chili)
- Shredded radicchio with melted mozzarella cheese
- Mozzarella cheese melted over prosciutto, topped with fresh sage leaves
- Mozzarella cheese melted over chopped calamata olives and arugula

Red Bean Dip

I intended to make black bean hummus and drained dark red beans instead of black. Since I was (as usual) incredibly hurried and harried, I decided to proceed anyway. A perfect combination of spicy, sweet and salty, it has since become one of my favorite dips.

I recently came across chipotle chili powder in a Penzey's catalog (see page 21) and now I am hooked. You can use it anywhere you might use cayenne pepper but the chipotle (smoked jalapeño pepper) lends a wonderful smoky flavor.

Makes about 1½–2 cups

> *one 19-ounce can dark red kidney beans, drained and rinsed*
> *2 garlic cloves*
> *½ teaspoon ground cumin*
> *½ teaspoon chipotle chili powder or cayenne pepper*
> *1 teaspoon kosher salt*
> *¼ cup orange juice*
> *juice of ½ lime*
> *1 tablespoon chopped fresh cilantro leaves, for garnish*

Place the beans, garlic, cumin, chili powder and salt in a food processor fitted with a steel blade and process until smooth. Add the orange juice and lime juice and process until smooth.

Transfer to a serving bowl and serve immediately or cover and refrigerate up to 3 days. Garnish with the cilantro.

BRUSCHETTA
AND
DIPS

Artichoke and Feta Dip

Don't process this dip by machine; it's best left chunky.

Makes 1–1½ cups

1 can marinated artichoke hearts, drained and coarsely chopped
2 garlic cloves, minced
1 anchovy fillet, minced
½ cup sour cream or plain low-fat yogurt (do not use nonfat)
¼ cup crumbled feta cheese
¼ teaspoon black pepper
¼ teaspoon kosher salt
1 teaspoon chopped fresh dill, plus additional whole stems for garnish

Place all the ingredients in a small mixing bowl and gently combine. Transfer to a small serving bowl and serve immediately or cover and re–frigerate up to 4 hours. Garnish with the additional dill.

CHUTNEY CREAM CHEESE

Chutney cream cheese is a nice change from typical savory dips. Sweet and spicy, it's great scooped up by celery stalks or endive leaves or paired with smoked turkey in a sandwich. The optional curry powder is a delicious but nonessential addition.

MAKES ABOUT 1–1¼ CUPS

> *½ pound cream cheese, at room temperature*
> *½ cup chutney, any kind will do*
> *1 teaspoon curry powder (optional)*
> *1 scallion, finely chopped, for garnish*

Place the cream cheese in a small mixing bowl and mash with a fork. Gradually add the chutney and curry powder, if desired, and mash until it is well incorporated.

Transfer to a small serving bowl and serve immediately or cover and refrigerate up to 3 days. Garnish with the scallion.

BRUSCHETTA AND DIPS

Gorgonzola Dip

A wonderfully rich and creamy dip that can be scooped up with endive leaves, pea pods or asparagus, stuffed into cherry tomatoes, swirled into mashed potatoes or dolloped on grilled steak.

Makes 1¼ cups

> *¼ pound Gorgonzola cheese, at room temperature*
> *¼ pound cream cheese, at room temperature*
> *¼ cup heavy or light cream*
> *4 tablespoons toasted walnuts, chopped (see page 102)*
> *1 teaspoon cognac*

Place the Gorgonzola and cream cheese in a small mixing bowl and mash with a fork. Gradually add the cream, 1 tablespoon at a time, 3 tablespoons of the walnuts and cognac and mash until well incorporated.

Transfer to a small serving bowl and serve immediately or cover and refrigerate up to 3 days. Garnish with the remaining 1 tablespoon walnuts.

Roasted Red Pepper Dip with Walnuts and Pomegranate Molasses

This is a combination of several different recipes, most of them Turkish in origin. While I usually serve it with pita triangles, it is also great dolloped on grilled chicken.

Roasting red peppers is an incredibly easy task and one that you can do well ahead of time, but if you must, feel free to use a high-quality canned roasted red pepper. Just be sure to rinse them off well.

Pomegranate molasses, readily available at Middle Eastern specialty food stores, is the boiled down juice of pomegranate seeds, and although it's unsweetened, it's very, very intense. I love the flavor, although it is not something that I use a lot in my cooking. Then, one cold winter night when my friend Lizzy Shaw was visiting from LA, she and my husband Mark concocted a Fizzy Lizzy: one shot of Vodka, 1 teaspoon pomegranate molasses and ice and soda water to fill a 12-ounce glass. Lime garnish optional.

3 red bell peppers (substitute yellow, orange or purple, but don't even consider green)
1 tablespoon olive oil
1 Spanish onion, chopped
2 garlic cloves, chopped
1 tablespoon light brown sugar
1 cup toasted walnuts, chopped (see page 102)
1 tablespoon ground cumin
juice of 1 lime
2 tablespoons pomegranate molasses
2–3 tablespoons chopped fresh Italian flat-leaf parsley leaves, for garnish

continued on next page

BRUSCHETTA AND DIPS

Roasted Red Pepper Dip with Walnuts and Pomegranate Molasses (*cont.*)

Preheat the broiler.

Remove the top and bottom of each pepper and slice it open, so that you end up with a flat rectangular shaped sheet of pepper. Discard the seeds. Place the peppers, skin side up, directly under the broiler, as close together as possible and cook until blackened, about 5 to 7 minutes. Transfer to a heavy plastic or paper bag and let sweat for about 10 minutes. Discard the burned skin and set the peppers aside.

Place a large skillet over medium–high heat and when it is hot, add the oil. Add the onion, garlic and brown sugar and cook until the onion is slightly caramelized, about 10 minutes. Transfer to a food processor fitted with a steel blade and add the reserved peppers, walnuts, cumin, lime juice and pomegranate molasses and puree until smooth.

Transfer to a small serving bowl, cover and refrigerate at least 1 hour and up to 2 days. Garnish with the parsley.

Caramelized Onion Dip

I can barely cut an onion without thinking of the parade of high school girls who worked at From the Night Kitchen. Every weekday some combination of girls (Erin, Daphne, Michelle, just to name a few) arrived at my store promptly (yeah, right) at 3:30 P.M., donned swimming goggles and hand–cut 50–pound bags of Spanish onions for the huge quantities of soup we made daily.

My favorite way to cut scallions is with poultry shears. I find that I often can't cut all the way through the stalks with a knife, even one that has been newly sharpened.

Makes about 1–1¼ cups

> 1 tablespoon olive oil
>
> 1 tablespoon unsalted butter
>
> 1 large or 2 small red onions, thinly sliced
>
> 1 teaspoon chopped fresh rosemary leaves
>
> ½ cup sour cream
>
> ½ cup mayonnaise
>
> ¼ teaspoon kosher salt
>
> ¼ teaspoon black pepper
>
> pinch cayenne pepper
>
> 1 scallion green, chopped, for garnish

To caramelize the onions: Place a small skillet over low heat and when it is hot, add the oil and butter. Add the onions and rosemary and cook, stirring occasionally, until the onions are deeply browned and caramelized, about 35 to 40 minutes. Transfer to a small mixing bowl and

continued on next page

Bruschetta and Dips

Caramelized Onion Dip (*cont.*)

let cool. (You can caramelize the onions a day or two ahead. They are great served on burgers, sandwiches and omelettes.)

Add the sour cream, mayonnaise, salt, pepper and cayenne to the cooled onions and mix to combine.

Transfer to a small serving bowl and serve immediately or cover and refrigerate up to 2 days. Garnish with the scallion green.

HERB CHEESE

Herb Cheese, like its inspiration, Boursin Cheese, is so versatile it's worth having some around all the time. You can use it with crudités, crackers and breadsticks, but my favorite is to stuff it inside a burger or pair it with roast beef or ham in a sandwich. It's also great added to scrambled eggs at the last minute.

> 1 pound cream cheese, at room temperature (do not use nonfat)
> ¼–½ cup buttermilk
> 1–2 garlic cloves, finely chopped
> 3 tablespoons finely chopped fresh parsley leaves, plus additional for garnish
> 1 tablespoon finely chopped fresh basil leaves or 1 teaspoon dried basil
> 1 teaspoon finely chopped fresh oregano leaves or ⅓ teaspoon dried oregano
> ½ teaspoon dried thyme
> ½ teaspoon black pepper

Place the cream cheese in a small mixing bowl and mash with a fork. Gradually add the buttermilk and mash until it is well incorporated. Add the garlic, herbs and pepper and mix to combine.

Transfer to a small serving bowl and serve immediately or cover and refrigerate up to 3 days. Garnish with the additional parsley.

BRUSCHETTA AND DIPS

SPICY SESAME DIP

At first the combination of Asian ingredients and mayonnaise struck me as very bizarre, but I tried it anyway and discovered a great treat. It's especially good with pea pods, asparagus and bell peppers or mixed into cooked and cooled spaghetti.

MAKES ABOUT 1¾–2 CUPS

2 garlic cloves
2 teaspoons Dijon mustard
¼–½ teaspoon cayenne pepper
1 teaspoon chili powder
½ cup cooled, brewed tea
2 tablespoons red wine vinegar
1½ tablespoons soy sauce
½ cup tahini (sesame seed paste) (you can substitute peanut
  or cashew butter)
1 cup mayonnaise
1 scallion green, finely chopped, for garnish

Place the garlic in a food processor fitted with a steel blade and process until chopped. Add the mustard, cayenne and chili powder and process for 30 seconds. While the machine is still running, gradually add the tea, vinegar, soy sauce, tahini and mayonnaise and process until completely smooth.

Transfer to a small serving bowl, cover and refrigerate at least 1 hour and up to 2 days. Garnish with the scallion green.

Chickpea Spread

You can vary this spread by adding chopped or pureed cilantro, basil, roasted bell peppers or chili peppers, olives (any kind will do), scallions, chives or lemon, lime or orange zest.

Makes about 1¼ cups

> 1 16-ounce can chickpeas, drained and rinsed
> 1–2 garlic cloves, finely chopped
> 2 tablespoons extra-virgin olive oil
> 3 tablespoons fresh lemon juice
> ½ teaspoon ground cumin, or more to taste
> ½ teaspoon Hungarian paprika, plus additional for garnish
> 1 teaspoon soy sauce, or more to taste
> ½ teaspoon kosher salt
> ¼–½ teaspoon black pepper
> lemon, lime or orange slices, for garnish

Place the chickpeas and garlic in a food processor fitted with a steel blade and process until smooth. While the machine is still running, grad–ually add the oil, lemon juice, cumin, paprika, soy sauce, salt and pepper and process until completely smooth.

Transfer to a small serving bowl and serve immediately or cover and refrigerate up to 2 days. Garnish with the additional paprika and lemon slices.

Bruschetta and Dips

Basic Salsa

Your basic salsa. Serve with chips or on burgers and omelettes.

Makes about 2 cups

> 1–1½ pounds beefsteak tomatoes, seeded, if desired, and diced
> ½ red onion, coarsely chopped
> 1–2 garlic cloves, chopped
> 1 yellow bell pepper, coarsely chopped
> ½ jalapeño pepper or chipotle chile, seeded, if desired, and finely chopped
> ¼ cup finely chopped fresh cilantro leaves
> ½ teaspoon cayenne pepper
> ¼ teaspoon kosher salt
> 1 tablespoon fresh lime juice

Place all the ingredients in a medium-size serving bowl, mix to combine, cover and refrigerate at least 3 to 4 hours and up to 8 hours.

GUACAMOLE

Be sure to buy avocados well ahead of when you want them; you can rarely find them ripe. To hasten the ripening process, place the avocado in a paper bag with an apple; it's ready when you can push it in slightly. If it's already ripe enough, simply refrigerate it; it won't continue to ripen in the fridge.

I never ate, or even heard of an avocado until I was fifteen. Then my parents went away and asked their twenty-something friends Judy Nissenbaum and Ian Dove to stay with me and my two brothers, Thomas and Peter.

Left in a larger and more grown up apartment than they were used to, Judy and Ian had twelve people over for brunch and served avocado drizzled with a very vinegar-y vinaigrette. I can still remember the buttery, nutty taste. I was hooked and ate avocado halves drizzled with vinegar-y vinaigrette at every opportunity. It was not until years later that I could even consider another treatment. This dip is a close match, and is also great in sandwiches and omelettes.

MAKES 3–4 CUPS

> 4 perfectly ripe Haas avocados, coarsely chopped
> 1 small beefsteak tomato, coarsely chopped
> 2 scallions, chopped
> ½ cup chopped fresh cilantro leaves
> 1 pinch cayenne pepper
> ¼–⅓ teaspoon kosher salt
> ⅛ teaspoon crushed red pepper flakes
> 1½ tablespoons fresh lime juice (about 1 lime)
> ½ jalapeño pepper or chipotle chile, finely minced (optional)
> 5 cilantro sprigs, for garnish
> 2 very thin slices lime, for garnish

continued on next page

BRUSCHETTA AND DIPS

Guacamole (*cont.*)

Place all the ingredients in a medium-size mixing bowl and toss gently to mix. Do not overmix; it should be somewhat chunky.

Transfer to a medium-size serving bowl and serve immediately or place a few pits in the guacamole (to prevent discoloration), cover tightly and refrigerate up to 8 hours. Garnish with the cilantro and lime slices.

TSATSIKI

This sauce, with the consistency of a salad, can be found in slight variations in almost every Middle Eastern country. I first had it in Greece where they made it with very thick yogurt, so I always drain the yogurt first. This method does require some forethought: The yogurt needs to sit overnight to reach the right consistency. It is a great dip for pita bread or crudités.

MAKES ABOUT 1½ CUPS

> *1 quart lowfat or full-fat plain yogurt (do not use nonfat)*
> *cheesecloth*
> *1–2 cucumbers, peeled, seeded, halved and thinly sliced or diced*
> *2 garlic cloves, minced*
> *1 tablespoon finely chopped fresh mint leaves*
> *¼–½ teaspoon kosher salt*
> *2 fresh mint leaves, for garnish*

Line a colander with cheesecloth or muslin. Place the colander over a large mixing bowl. Place the yogurt in the colander, cover and refrigerate overnight.

Discard the liquid that has drained into the bowl and transfer the yogurt to a small mixing bowl. Add the cucumber, garlic, mint and salt and mix to combine. Transfer to a small serving bowl and serve immediately or cover and refrigerate up to 2 days. Garnish with the mint.

BRUSCHETTA AND DIPS

FAVA BEAN DIP

The inspiration for this dip came from Lydia Shire and Susan Regis of Boston's Biba restaurant. Easy and unexpected, it is best served with bread or breadsticks.

MAKES ABOUT 1 CUP

> 1 cup fresh fava or lima beans, shelled
> 4 garlic cloves, chopped
> ¼ cup extra-virgin olive oil
> 1 tablespoon fresh lemon juice
> ½ teaspoon black pepper
> ½ teaspoon kosher salt
> 2–4 very thin slices of fresh lemon, for garnish
> 2 large fresh basil leaves, cut in slivers, for garnish

Place a large bowl of ice water on the counter.

Bring a large pot of water to a boil over very high heat. Add the beans and cook until they turn bright green, about 2 minutes. Place the beans in the ice bath and drain.

Place the beans and garlic in a food processor fitted with a steel blade and puree. While the machine is running, gradually add the oil, lemon juice, pepper and salt.

Transfer to a small serving bowl and serve immediately or cover and refrigerate up to 2 days. Garnish with the lemon slices and basil.

MENU ONE

MOROCCAN CHICKEN
FRESH HERB COUSCOUS
RED ONION AND BLOOD ORANGE SALAD
CHOCOLATE DATE NUT BARS

Like many Moroccan and Moroccan–inspired meals, this one is infused with rich and full flavors. If you prefer, you can substitute roasted potatoes, soft polenta or steamed rice. And although your house will be filled with wonderful aromas, this meal is deceptively simple to prepare.

Much of the preparation can be done ahead of time.

TIME TIPS:

MAKE THE CHOCOLATE DATE NUT BARS THE DAY BEFORE.

MARINATE THE CHICKEN.

MAKE THE RED ONION AND BLOOD ORANGE SALAD AND THE DRESSING IN THE AFTERNOON BUT DO NOT COMBINE THEM UNTIL JUST BEFORE SERVING.

START COOKING THE COUSCOUS JUST BEFORE YOU LOWER THE HEAT ON THE CHICKEN.

Moroccan Chicken

Sweet and spicy, with the traditional combination of poultry and fruit flavors.

Note: If you want to hold the chicken in the oven, omit the last step and instead of finishing the chicken in the skillet, finish it in the oven, at 300 degrees for 12 to 15 minutes.

6 boneless chicken breast halves, excess fat removed (about 3 pounds)
2 tablespoons olive oil
½ cup fresh orange juice
3 garlic cloves, minced
½ teaspoon cayenne pepper
1 tablespoon ground cinnamon
¾ teaspoon ground cumin
1 tablespoon chili powder
1 teaspoon light brown sugar
1 teaspoon kosher salt
½ teaspoon black pepper
½ cup black olives, such as Kalamata or oil-cured
½–1 cup chicken broth
¼ cup chopped fresh Italian flat-leaf parsley leaves, for garnish

Place the chicken, oil, orange juice, garlic, cayenne, cinnamon, cumin, chili powder and sugar in a large glass or ceramic bowl. Cover and refrigerate for at least 2 hours and no longer than 8. Dry the chicken and reserve the marinade.

Sprinkle the chicken with the salt and pepper. Place a large nonstick skillet over medium–high heat and when it is hot, add the chicken breasts, skin side down, one at a time, allowing the pan to reheat for about 30 seconds between additions. Cook until deeply browned, about 3 minutes on each side, basting all the while. Lower the heat to medium-low and cook until the chicken is fully cooked, about 5 to 7 minutes, turning occasionally. Transfer the chicken to a heated serving platter.

Reheat the skillet, add the olives, remaining marinade and the chicken broth and bring to a boil. Pour over the chicken and serve immediately. Garnish with the parsley.

MENU
ONE

FRESH HERB COUSCOUS

*L*ike pasta in Italy and rice in Asia, couscous is a staple in Morocco.

½ teaspoon kosher salt

1 tablespoon finely chopped fresh cilantro leaves

2 tablespoons finely chopped fresh basil leaves

2 tablespoons toasted sesame seeds

2½ cups boiling water

2 cups couscous

1 tablespoon unsalted butter, at room temperature (optional)

Place the salt, cilantro, 1 tablespoon basil and sesame seeds in a small mixing bowl, toss to combine and set aside.

Place the water and couscous in a large mixing bowl, cover and let sit for 5 minutes. Add the herb mixture and if desired, the butter, and gently mix.

Transfer to a heated serving bowl and serve immediately. Garnish with the remaining 1 tablespoon basil.

Red Onion and Blood Orange Salad

*S*weet, tart, salty, crunchy and soft, this salad combines many flavors and textures. It can be served as a starter or after the meal.

1 large red onion, thinly sliced or chopped

2 blood oranges, thinly sliced or chopped

2 tablespoons olive oil

1 tablespoon plus 1 teaspoon balsamic vinegar

½–⅔ cup toasted pine nuts (see page 102)

½ teaspoon kosher salt

¼–½ teaspoon black pepper

about 6 cups mesclun greens

Place the red onion, oranges, oil, vinegar, pine nuts, salt and pepper in a medium-size mixing bowl and toss gently.

Divide the mesclun greens among 6 salad plates and top each with an equal amount of salad. Serve immediately.

MENU
ONE

CHOCOLATE DATE NUT BARS

When I owned From the Night Kitchen, one of my employees suggested making these. They were not only absolutely delicious, but were one of our best sellers and something that couldn't be found anywhere else.

1 cup dates, finely chopped

½ cup boiling water

1 ounce unsweetened chocolate, chopped

½ cup unsalted butter, at room temperature

1 cup sugar

2 large eggs

½ teaspoon vanilla extract

1¼ cups all-purpose flour

2 tablespoons unsweetened cocoa powder

½ teaspoon kosher salt

1 teaspoon baking soda

For the Topping:

⅓ cup sugar

½ cup chopped pecans or walnuts

½ cup semisweet chocolate chips

Preheat the oven to 325 degrees. Lightly butter a 9 x 12–inch baking pan.

Place the dates, boiling water and chocolate in a small bowl, stir to combine and set aside to cool.

Place the butter and sugar in a medium–size mixing bowl and blend until creamy. Add the eggs, one at a time, stirring well after each addition, and vanilla extract and blend until fully incorporated. Add the flour, cocoa powder, salt and baking soda and mix until thoroughly combined.

When the date mixture is cool, add it to the flour mixture and mix until thoroughly combined. Pour it into the prepared pan.

To make the topping: Place the sugar, nuts and chips in a small mixing bowl and stir until combined. Sprinkle evenly over the date mixture and transfer the pan to the oven.

Bake until a cake tester comes out clean, about 25 minutes. Set aside to cool and cut into 12 pieces. Transfer to a platter and serve immediately or cool, cover and store at room temperature overnight.

MENU
ONE

Menu Two

Caribbean Spiced Chicken
Coconut Black Bean Risotto
Cucumber Salad with Yogurt and Mint
Key Lime Mousse with Toasted Coconut

This dish was inspired by a recipe card I saw in a magazine for a dish of long-grain rice with chicken and black beans on the side. At first glance, the combination looks unusual, but chicken, beans and rice are a traditional combination in many different cuisines. This dish uses an abundance of herbs and spices, and while it tastes lavish, spicy and exotic, it is still very down to earth. The coconut risotto takes it even one step further into the sublime.

TIME TIPS:

In the afternoon:

Toast the coconut (some for the risotto and some for the mousse).

Marinate the chicken.

Chop the risotto ingredients.

Make the Key Lime Mousse.

CARIBBEAN SPICED CHICKEN

Either loved or abhorred, cilantro is a controversial herb. It has been praised as an aphrodisiac, lauded as a remedy for nosebleeds and compared to the smell of bedbugs and rubber. The leaf, which looks like flat-leaf parsley, is traditionally used in Mexican, Thai, Indian, Middle Eastern and Portuguese cooking. It is best known for its appearance in salsa, guacamole, beans and curried dishes. It is especially great paired with mint.

Buy cilantro only when it is very fresh; it should be bright and curly. To store, place the stems in a glass of cold water and cover the leaves with a plastic bag; it should keep for about a week. Wash it just before using. Never, ever substitute dried coriander for fresh cilantro leaves.

6 skinless, boneless chicken breast halves, thinly pounded to an even thickness, excess fat and tenders removed
¼ cup chopped fresh cilantro leaves
2 tablespoons chopped fresh mint leaves
2 tablespoons fresh gingerroot, peeled, if desired
5 garlic cloves
½–1 teaspoon cayenne pepper
1 tablespoon dried Greek oregano
1 teaspoon ground cinnamon
2 teaspoons dried thyme
2 tablespoons coriander
2 tablespoons olive oil
juice and zest of 1 lime

1½ teaspoons kosher salt
½ teaspoon black pepper
6 cilantro sprigs, for garnish
6 mint leaves, for garnish
1 lime, thinly sliced, for garnish

Place the chicken breasts in a large glass or ceramic bowl.

Place the cilantro, mint, gingerroot and garlic in the bowl of a food processor fitted with a steel blade and pulse until chopped. Add the cayenne, oregano, cinnamon, thyme and coriander and pulse until the spices have been incorporated.

While the machine is running, gradually add the oil and lime juice and zest and combine until it forms a paste. Rub into the chicken. Cover and refrigerate up to 4 hours but no longer than 8.

Sprinkle the chicken with the salt and pepper. Heat the skillet over a medium–high heat and when it is hot, add the chicken breasts, skin side down, one at a time, allowing the pan to reheat for about 30 seconds between additions. You do not need to add additional oil, there's enough in the rub. Cook until the chicken is deeply browned and the juices run clear, about 5 to 7 minutes on each side. Transfer the chicken to a heated large serving platter and serve immediately. Garnish with the cilantro, mint and lime.

MENU
TWO

Coconut Black Bean Risotto

*A*lthough this sounds like an odd combination of Italian technique and Caribbean ingredients, it tastes absolutely wonderful. You can also serve this as a vegetarian entrée. Start the risotto about 10 minutes before you start the chicken.

> *¼ cup unsweetened shredded coconut, for garnish*
> *1 tablespoon unsalted butter or olive oil*
> *½ Spanish onion, minced*
> *4 garlic cloves, minced*
> *2 cups arborio rice*
> *1 cup white wine*
> *6–7 cups chicken or vegetable broth*
> *¼ cup crumbled feta or goat cheese*
> *¼ cup freshly grated Parmesan cheese*
> *⅓–½ cup chopped fresh cilantro leaves*
> *2 roasted red bell peppers, chopped (see page 38)*
> *1½ cups cooked black beans, drained and rinsed*

Place a large nonstick skillet over medium heat and when it is hot, add the coconut. Cook, shaking the pan occasionally, until the coconut is golden, about 10 minutes. Transfer to a small plate and set aside.

Place a large straight-sided pan over medium heat and when it is hot, add the butter. Add the onion and garlic and cook until the onion is translucent, about 4 to 5 minutes. Add the rice and stir until it is coated with the onion mixture. Add the wine and cook until it has been completely absorbed.

Add the chicken broth, one cup at a time, and cook until all the broth has been absorbed by the rice, about 18 minutes.

Off heat, add the cheeses, cilantro, peppers and beans. Transfer to a large heated serving bowl and serve immediately. Garnish with the toasted coconut.

MENU
TWO

Cucumber Salad with Yogurt and Mint

*I*t's easy to forget the lowly cucumber, which is so often hidden in salads of tasteless iceberg lettuce. Here, paired with yogurt and mint, it's a refreshing contrast to the chicken.

3 cucumbers, peeled, seeded if desired, and thinly sliced

½ red onion, thinly sliced

4–5 tablespoons plain yogurt

4 teaspoons red wine vinegar

1 heaping tablespoon chopped fresh mint leaves

½ teaspoon kosher salt

⅛–¼ teaspoon white pepper

Combine all the ingredients in a medium–size serving bowl. Serve immediately.

Key Lime Mousse
with Toasted Coconut

You may have to search specialty stores for key lime juice, which is not inexpensive, but if you like this tart and creamy dessert, it's well worth it. Key Lime Mousse can be whipped up in minutes. Without the more commonly served crust of key lime pie, my friend Nancy Olin describes this as intensely flavored, lime whipped cream.

This is also excellent served with fresh berries.

> **Key lime juice can be substituted for fresh lemon or lime juice in most dessert recipes but not the other way around. Don't use fresh lime juice in this recipe; it will lack the proper intensity of flavor.**

¼ cup unsweetened shredded coconut, for garnish
4 large egg yolks
6 tablespoons sugar
½ cup plus 2 tablespoons key lime juice
2 cups heavy cream
zest of one lime, cut into thin strips, for garnish

Place a large nonstick skillet over medium heat and when it is hot, add the coconut. Cook, shaking the pan occasionally, until the coconut is golden, about 10 minutes. Transfer to a small plate and set aside.

Place a large copper or stainless steel bowl in the freezer.

Place the egg yolks, sugar and key lime juice in a double boiler. Bring

continued on next page

Menu Two

Key Lime Mousse with Toasted Coconut (*cont.*)

the water to a boil over high heat and cook until the egg mixture begins to thicken, about 5 minutes. Set aside to cool to room temperature.

Remove the bowl from the freezer and add the cream. With a whisk or an electric beater, beat the cream until it forms soft peaks. Gradually fold in the egg mixture. Transfer to chilled individual serving bowls or wine glasses and serve immediately or cover and refrigerate up to 4 hours. Serve garnished with the lime and reserved toasted coconut.

MENU THREE

ROSEMARY OREGANO LAMB BURGERS
ROAST POTATOES WITH FETA CHEESE
ROMAINE WITH CUCUMBERS AND TOMATOES
FRESH FRUIT WITH BERRY PUREE

*A*lthough beef burgers don't seem special enough to serve at a dinner party, I wouldn't hesitate to serve these Greek–inspired lamb burgers. Rustic and intriguingly spiced, these are great cooked on either a grill or a cast–iron pan.

Be sure to use a good quality Greek olive oil: it is included in every course (except dessert). Start this meal with a big bowl of green and black olives, a bowl of hummus and a bowl of Tsatsiki (see page 47), lots of toasted pita bread and crudités. You could also start with Avgolemono soup (see page 124).

TIME TIPS:

THE BURGERS CAN BE ASSEMBLED, COVERED AND REFRIGERATED UP TO 8 HOURS AHEAD.

THE FIRST 4 INGREDIENTS OF ROAST POTATOES WITH FETA CHEESE CAN BE MIXED UP TO 4 HOURS AHEAD.

THE SALAD INGREDIENTS AND THE DRESSING CAN BE ASSEMBLED BUT NOT COMBINED UP TO 4 HOURS AHEAD.

THE BERRY PUREE CAN BE MADE AND REFRIGERATED UP TO 2 DAYS AHEAD.

Rosemary Oregano Lamb Burgers

A modern version of the old burger standby, Lamb Burgers are incredibly quick and easy to make and take almost no time to cook. In addition, they can be made ahead of time, frozen raw, and then defrosted when needed. Try serving these inside small pita breads.

> *2–2½ pounds ground lamb*
> *3 garlic cloves, minced*
> *1½ teaspoons Dijon mustard*
> *¼ cup chopped fresh mint leaves*
> *3 tablespoons chopped fresh rosemary leaves*
> *3 tablespoons chopped fresh Italian flat-leaf parsley leaves*
> *1 tablespoon dried Greek oregano*
> *¼–½ teaspoon cayenne pepper*
> *1½ teaspoons kosher salt*
> *1 teaspoon black pepper*
> *6 Kaiser rolls, toasted*

Place the lamb, garlic, mustard, mint, rosemary, parsley, oregano, cayenne, ½ teaspoon salt and ½ teaspoon pepper in a large mixing bowl and gently mix. Divide the meat into 6 balls of equal size and form into patties.

Sprinkle the burgers with the remaining 1 teaspoon salt and ½ teaspoon pepper. Place a large nonstick or cast-iron skillet over a medium-high heat and when it is hot, add the burgers, one at a time, allowing the pan to reheat for about 30 seconds between additions. Cook until medium well done, about 4 to 5 minutes on each side. Place the burgers on the rolls, pile on a large platter and serve immediately.

THE
$50
DINNER
PARTY

Roast Potatoes with Feta Cheese

*T*odd English, with whom I wrote *The Olives Table*, is without question the most talented chef I know. I have never had better food than that cooked by him and thankfully, after a year of testing his recipes, I have been hugely influenced. This recipe was inspired by his recipe for roast carrots with feta cheese.

> *2½–3 pounds new potatoes, cut into quarters*
> *1 tablespoon olive oil*
> *1 teaspoon kosher salt*
> *½ teaspoon black pepper*
> *2–3 tablespoons chopped fresh Italian flat-leaf parsley leaves*
> *½–¾ cup crumbled feta cheese*

Preheat the oven to 400 degrees.

Place the potatoes, oil, salt and pepper on a large baking sheet and toss to combine. Transfer to the oven and roast until the potatoes are well browned, about 40 minutes.

Add the parsley and feta, toss and transfer to a heated medium-size serving bowl. Serve immediately.

MENU
THREE

ROMAINE WITH CUCUMBERS AND TOMATOES

A cheeseless, oliveless version of the classic Greek salad. (You can find the cheese in the potatoes.) If you want to make a more traditional Greek salad, omit the feta cheese from the potatoes and add it to the salad, or if you love feta, put it in both.

> *2 heads romaine lettuce, well washed and torn into bite-size pieces*
> *2–3 beefsteak tomatoes, diced*
> *1–2 cucumbers, peeled, seeded if desired, and chopped*
> *1 red onion, thinly sliced*
>
> **For the Dressing:**
> *2 tablespoons olive oil*
> *2 tablespoons fresh lemon juice*
> *2 teaspoons dried Greek oregano*
> *½ teaspoon kosher salt*
> *¼ teaspoon black pepper*
> *½ cup crumbled feta cheese (optional)*

Place the romaine, tomatoes, cucumbers and red onion in a large salad bowl and toss to combine.

To make the dressing: Place the oil, lemon juice, oregano, salt and pepper in a small mixing bowl and whisk together. Pour over the salad, gently toss and sprinkle with the feta cheese if desired. Serve immediately.

FRESH FRUIT WITH BERRY PUREE

*F*resh fruit with fresh fruit sauce: what could be more disciplined?

> *1½ cups fresh or defrosted frozen raspberries*
> *1 tablespoon fresh lemon juice*
> *2 kiwis, each cut into 6 slices*
> *6 fresh figs*
> *2 blood oranges, cut into segments*

Place the raspberries and lemon juice in a food processor fitted with a steel blade and process until smooth. Transfer to a strainer and push out the liquid with the back of a wooden spoon into a small bowl. Discard the seeds. If necessary, add a little bit of water to thin out the puree.

Divide the puree between six plates or large wine glasses and top with the fruit.

NOTE: if you can't find the recommended fruits or don't like them, simply substitute your favorites.

MENU
THREE

MENU FOUR

CURRIED SWORDFISH WITH CILANTRO PASTE
OVEN-BAKED CORN
SAUTÉED CHERRY TOMATOES
STRAWBERRY RHUBARB COMPOTE

This dinner is the essence of summer. A little bit different (baking the corn instead of steaming it), a little bit exotic (cilantro paste on the fish), the meal is as delicious as it is homey.

Make this twist on the classic American barbecue when you have guests coming and you don't have a lot of time; it's appropriate for a weeknight meal as well as an elegant dinner party. The curry rub adds immeasurable flavor to the sword-fish; rub it into the swordfish when you get home. Read your mail, feed the kids, it's not important how long it sits.

TIME TIPS:

MAKE THE CURRY RUB FOR THE SWORDFISH UP TO 2 WEEKS AHEAD.

MAKE THE CILANTRO PASTE UP TO 3 DAYS AHEAD.

HUSK AND CLEAN THE CORN IN THE AFTERNOON.

PLACE THE CURRY RUB ON THE SWORDFISH IN THE AFTERNOON.

PREPARE AND COOK THE STRAWBERRY RHUBARB COMPOTE IN THE AFTERNOON. REHEAT IT LATER.

CURRIED SWORDFISH WITH CILANTRO PASTE

Delicate in flavor and meaty in texture, swordfish is my favorite fish.

For the Curry Rub:

1½ teaspoons curry powder

1½ teaspoons ground cumin

¾ teaspoon ground ginger

¾ teaspoon chili powder

1½ teaspoons kosher salt

½ teaspoon black pepper

For the Cilantro Paste:

¾–1 cup fresh cilantro leaves

1 garlic clove

1 heaping tablespoon pine nuts

¼ teaspoon kosher salt

1 tablespoon fresh lime juice

2 tablespoons extra-virgin olive oil

2 teaspoons olive oil

3–3½ pounds swordfish

To make the curry rub: Place the curry powder, cumin, ginger, chili powder, salt and pepper in a small mixing bowl, combine and rub into the swordfish. Cover and refrigerate up to 4 hours.

To make the cilantro paste: Place the cilantro, garlic, pine nuts and salt in a food processor fitted with a steel blade and process for 2 minutes, scraping down the sides of the bowl if necessary. While the machine is running, gradually add the lime juice and extra-virgin olive oil. Set aside.

Place a large skillet over medium–high heat and when it is hot, add the olive oil. Add the swordfish, one piece at a time, allowing the pan to reheat for about 30 seconds between additions. Cook until golden brown, about 4 to 5 minutes per side, depending upon the thickness. Divide between 6 heated plates and top each with a tablespoon of Cilantro Paste.

MENU
FOUR

Oven-Baked Corn

*I*f you've only had steamed or boiled corn on the cob, you're in for a real treat. Roasting, which is my favorite method, yields a corn that is a drier yet both sweeter and crunchier than steaming. I had never eaten it until my husband, Mark, surprised me by making dinner. I rarely eat it any other way now.

I suggest using nine ears of corn because I find that if I make six it's not enough, and if I make twelve it's too much. Feel free to make as much or as little as you and your guests will eat.

> *9 ears corn, husked and cleaned of the silk*
> *1–2 tablespoons olive oil or unsalted butter, at room temperature*
> *1 teaspoon kosher salt*
> *½ teaspoon black pepper*

Preheat the oven to 450 degrees.

Place the corn directly on the oven rack and cook until it is tender, about 12 minutes. Remove the corn from the oven, brush with the oil and sprinkle with the salt and pepper. Serve immediately.

Sautéed Cherry Tomatoes

I am a huge fan of cooked tomatoes. This method takes so little time but yields a great–tasting result.

> *2 teaspoons olive oil*
>
> *2 garlic cloves, finely chopped*
>
> *3 pints cherry tomatoes, halved (any combination of red and yellow is fine)*
>
> *1½ teaspoons chopped fresh rosemary, basil or oregano leaves or ¾ teaspoon dried rosemary, basil or oregano*
>
> *1 teaspoon kosher salt*
>
> *½ teaspoon black pepper*

Place a large skillet over low heat and when it is hot, add the oil. Add the garlic and cook until it just begins to turn golden, about 3 minutes. Raise the heat to medium, add the tomatoes and cook until they are tender and look withered, about 5 minutes. Add the rosemary, salt and pepper and cook for 1 minute. Transfer to a heated serving plate and serve immediately.

MENU
FOUR

STRAWBERRY RHUBARB COMPOTE

Strawberries and rhubarb are the most sublime combination. Here they are served unadulterated. If you must, add vanilla or ginger ice cream.

In Latin, *rhubarb* means "the root of the barbarians," meaning anything foreign or unknown. What it doesn't say is that the leaves are toxic, so be sure to use only the stalk. Most cookbooks recommend that you pull off the strings as you do for celery, but I find that using a vegetable peeler works even better.

> 5–6 cups chopped fresh or frozen rhubarb (about 3 pounds)
> ¼ cup sugar
> 5–6 cups fresh strawberries, hulled and quartered

Place the rhubarb and sugar in a medium-size saucepan and bring to a simmer over medium heat. Cook until the rhubarb is soft, about 20 minutes. Add the strawberries and cook until they turn pink, about 5 minutes.

Transfer to individual serving bowls and serve immediately or at room temperature.

MENU FIVE

CLASSIC LASAGNA
ROASTED GARLIC BREAD
SALAD OF ARUGULA, ENDIVE AND RADICCHIO
COOKIE PLATTER, GRAPES AND MELON

This Americanized classic Italian dinner is a perfect winter meal for good friends who don't need to be impressed with your kitchen wizardry. Whenever I make this meal, people are thrilled at being served something they wouldn't normally prepare themselves.

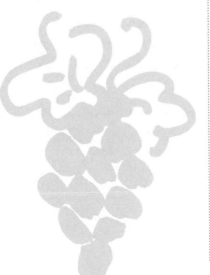

TIME TIPS:

PREPARE THE LASAGNA 2 DAYS BEFORE BUT DO NOT BAKE IT.

ONE DAY BEFORE, BAKE THE LASAGNA. REHEAT IT WHEN YOUR GUESTS ARRIVE.

MAKE THE GARLIC BUTTER UP TO ONE WEEK IN ADVANCE.

MAKE THE COOKIES UP TO 2 DAYS AHEAD.

Classic Lasagna

Although I didn't eat lasagna until I was in my twenties and only made it for the first time when I was in my thirties, it represents comfort to me. While a bad lasagna can be heavy, a good one is enriching, warm, substantial and yet light.

I like to serve lasagna straight from the baking pan, so be sure your pan is presentable but don't worry about a few drips down the sides.

If you are a vegetarian, you can substitute 1 medium eggplant, cubed for the sausage and 3 zucchini, cubed, for the beef.

For the Sauce:

1 tablespoon olive oil

1 Spanish onion, chopped

6 garlic cloves, minced

1 pound spicy or sweet Italian sausage or a combination of both, taken out of the casing and crumbled

1 pound ground beef

½ cup red wine

one 28-ounce can diced tomatoes

one 28-ounce can ground tomatoes

2 tablespoons tomato paste

1 teaspoon sugar

½ teaspoon crushed red pepper flakes (optional)

1 tablespoon dried Greek oregano

2 tablespoons dried basil

4 bay leaves

1 tablespoon fennel seed

For the Cheese Layer:

¾–1 pound ricotta cheese

2 large eggs

1½ cups finely grated Parmesan cheese

⅛ teaspoon nutmeg

¾ pound lasagna noodles, cooked and cooled, or no-boil type

⅔–¾ pound fontina cheese, thinly sliced or grated

⅓–½ cup chopped fresh basil leaves

To make the tomato sauce: Place a large skillet over medium heat and when it is hot, add the oil. Add the onion and garlic and cook until they are golden, about 3 minutes. Add the sausage and beef, or eggplant and zucchini, breaking them up with the back of a wooden spoon, and cook until they lose their rawness, about 7 to 10 minutes. Add the wine and cook until it has been absorbed by the meat, about 3 minutes. Lower the heat to low, add the tomatoes, tomato paste, sugar, red pepper flakes, if desired, oregano, basil, bay leaves and fennel and cook, partially covered, until it has thickened, about 2 to 3 hours. Remove the bay leaves.

While the sauce is cooking, prepare the cheese layer: Place the ricotta, eggs, 1 cup Parmesan cheese and nutmeg in a medium-size mixing bowl and combine.

To assemble the lasagna: Place 1 cup tomato sauce in an 8 x 13-inch pan. Top with a layer of noodles, ⅓ ricotta mixture, ⅓ fontina, ⅓ basil and 2½ cups sauce. Repeat two more times. Top with one layer noodles, 2½ cups sauce, one light layer fontina, and the remaining ½ cup Parmesan cheese. Cover with plastic wrap and press down, allowing the layers to tighten up. Refrigerate overnight.

Preheat the oven to 350 degrees.

MENU
FIVE

continued on next page

Classic Lasagna (*cont.*)

Remove the plastic wrap and transfer the lasagna to the oven. Bake until the cheese is lightly browned, about 40 minutes. Let cool about 20 minutes, cover with aluminum foil and refrigerate overnight.

Just prior to serving, preheat the oven to 350 degrees. Do not remove the foil. Place the lasagna in the oven and bake until warmed throughout, about 30 minutes.

Roasted Garlic Bread

I am not a fan of buttering bread, but for this I make an eager exception. In fact, I guarantee that people will eat so much, you might want to serve two long baguettes. You must use a really high quality unsalted butter (never salted) and either leave it out to warm to room temperature or whip it in a frenzy in a mixer (but be careful not to overwhip it to heavy cream).

After eating this butter on bread, I was sure that it would be equally delicious on spaghetti but I was absolutely wrong. The subtle flavor got quite lost.

People who are not accustomed to eating whole roasted garlic are often horrified when they see a recipe like this one. But the fear is for nothing, as this method makes for garlic that is sweet and mild. Always remove the green sprout found inside some garlic cloves; it's the most difficult part to digest, which makes the pungent flavor linger longest on your breath.

> *1 head garlic*
> *1 teaspoon olive oil*
> *½ cup unsalted butter, at room temperature*
> *¼ cup extra-virgin olive oil*
> *1 teaspoon chopped fresh basil leaves*
> *1 teaspoon chopped fresh Italian flat-leaf parsley leaves*
> *½ teaspoon dried Greek oregano*
> *½ teaspoon kosher salt*
> *1 French or Italian baguette, thickly sliced*

Preheat the oven to 450 degrees.

To roast the garlic: Remove as much of the paper from the garlic as possible, being careful to keep the head intact. Sprinkle with the olive oil and place in a small baking pan or on a large piece of aluminum foil.

continued on next page

MENU
FIVE

Roasted Garlic Bread (*cont.*)

Cook until the garlic is soft and tender, about 35 minutes. When cool enough to handle, remove the peel.

To make the garlic butter: Place the butter, extra–virgin olive oil and garlic in a small mixing bowl and mash with a fork. Add the basil, parsley, oregano and salt. Transfer to a small ramekin or serving bowl.

Just prior to serving, toast the bread slices. Place in a basket lined with a thick cloth napkin and serve immediately.

Salad of Arugula, Endive and Radicchio

*P*ungent smelling and bitter tasting, this is my favorite mixed salad, which I would pair with just about any entrée.

> 3 bunches arugula, well washed and torn
> 2 Belgian endives, leaves torn off and left whole
> 1 large head radicchio, torn
> ½ pound white mushrooms, trimmed and thinly sliced
> ¼ cup fresh lemon juice
> 3 tablespoons olive oil
> ½ teaspoon kosher salt
> ½ teaspoon black pepper

Place the arugula, endive, radicchio and mushrooms in a large salad bowl, drizzle with the lemon juice and oil and sprinkle with the salt and pepper. Serve immediately.

MENU
FIVE

Cookie Platter, Grapes and Melon

*A*ny combination of the cookies from pages 219–227 would be great with this meal, but if you have the inclination to make only one, I'd recommend the Cocoa Cookies (see page 220). Allow at least three to four cookies per person.

> *1 bunch green grapes*
> *1 bunch purple grapes*
> *1 cantaloupe, sliced*
> *18–24 cookies (see pages 219–227)*

Place the fruit in the center of a large platter and surround with the cookies.

*I*t always seemed to me that there could be nothing more wonderful than a roasted chicken dish that would be appropriate for a range of settings: an informal dinner for the family or a nicer, although not formal, dinner for guests, ranging from close friends to those I might not know well. As a result, I have become completely fanatical about this recipe. I have tried different cooking temperatures, different vegetables and even different kinds of chicken, from whole to cut-up pieces. I like this version. Paired with the broccoli rabe and orzo, this makes an easy and comforting dinner.

The amount of vegetables and fruit may look huge, but I have never served this and ended up with anything other than leftover chicken. Vary the vegetables to your taste. Almost any root vegetable will do, though sweet potatoes, turnips, rutabagas and celery root are particularly good.

TIME TIPS:

CUT THE VEGETABLES AND APPLES FOR THE CHICKEN AND PLACE IN A LARGE MIXING BOWL WITH THE OIL IN THE AFTERNOON.

COOK THE ORZO AND BROCCOLI RABE IN THE AFTERNOON BUT DO NOT COMBINE THEM.

ASSEMBLE BUT DO NOT BAKE THE BREAD PUDDING. BAKE IT WHILE YOU ARE EATING THE CHICKEN.

Garlic Roasted Chicken with Pan-Roasted Vegetables

You need a huge roasting pan, probably the one you only pull out at Thanksgiving. I like to serve this right out of the pan.

> **Note: if you want to use bone-in skin-on chicken breasts only instead of the whole chicken, place the chicken and vegetables together in the roasting pan and cook for 45 minutes instead of 1 hour.**

2 whole roaster chickens, about 5–6 pounds each, giblets and neck removed
¼ cup olive oil
6 garlic cloves, peeled
12 shallots, peeled (or 3 Spanish onions, quartered)
6–8 carrots, peeled, if desired, and cut into chunks
2 Idaho potatoes, unpeeled and cut into chunks
3 ripe pears or apples (any kind will do), peeled, if desired, and diced
1 butternut squash, peeled, seeded and cut into 1-inch cubes
1½ teaspoons dried sage
1 tablespoon kosher salt

Preheat the oven to 450 degrees.

Rinse the chickens in several changes of cold water and pat dry.

Place the oil, garlic, shallots, carrots, potatoes, pears or apples and butternut squash in a large mixing bowl and toss well.

Place the sage and salt in a small mixing bowl and mix to combine. Rub half into the chicken flesh, skin and cavity and sprinkle the other half on the vegetables.

Place the chicken on a roasting rack in a large roasting pan and sur-round it with the vegetables. Transfer to the oven and cook until the internal temperature reaches 160 degrees or the juices run clear from the breast and the leg moves easily, about 1 hour (about 10 minutes per pound). Serve immediately.

MENU
SIX

Orzo and Broccoli Rabe

*I*f you haven't tried broccoli rabe (also known as Italian broccoli, broccoli raab and broccoli di rape), this is a good introduction. The bitterness (which I love) overwhelms some people, but is somewhat lessened by the taste of the creamy orzo. I can't convince my husband to eat even this mild rendition, so I often eat it as an entrée when he goes out of town. It is especially good with shaved Parmesan cheese.

Assemble and cook the orzo and the broccoli rabe just before serving.

> *2 bunches broccoli rabe, trimmed and chopped*
> *¾–1 pound orzo*
> *1 tablespoon olive oil*
> *1 shallot, thinly sliced*
> *1 teaspoon kosher salt*
> *½ teaspoon black pepper*
> *¼–½ teaspoon crushed red pepper flakes (optional)*
> *2–4 tablespoons water*

Place the broccoli rabe in a large pan with 2 inches of water, cover and bring to a boil over high heat. Cook until the rabe is tender, about 7 to 10 minutes. Drain and set aside.

Place a large pot of water over high heat and when it comes to a boil, add the orzo. Cook until the orzo is tender, about 10 to 12 minutes. Drain and set aside.

Place a large skillet over medium–high heat and when it is hot, add the oil. Add the shallot and cook until it is golden, about 2 to 3 minutes. Add the orzo, broccoli rabe, salt, black pepper and if desired, the red pepper flakes, and the water and cook until the orzo and rabe are warmed throughout, about 3 minutes.

Transfer to a heated serving bowl and serve immediately.

Chocolate Bread Pudding Drizzled with Heavy Cream

I never tasted bread pudding until I made this one, which tastes like a very rich, very decadent brownie. Even if you don't usually serve heavy cream, don't omit it here: the pudding is at its best with something that contrasts with the chocolate intensity. You could also serve vanilla or cinnamon ice cream or whipped cream instead of the heavy cream.

Note: if you can find it, it's worth searching health food and specialty food stores for heavy cream that has not been ultra-pasteurized.

6 cups ½–1 inch bread cubes (from day-old anadama, oatmeal, challah, cinnamon, white bread or a combination)
1½ cups heavy cream
6 ounces semisweet chocolate, grated
2 ounces unsweetened chocolate, grated
½ cup sugar
5 large eggs, separated
⅓ cup unsalted butter, at room temperature
1 tablespoon vanilla extract
pinch kosher salt

Preheat the oven to 350 degrees. Lightly butter an 8 x 8–inch baking dish.

Place the bread cubes in a large mixing bowl. Place 1 cup cream in a small saucepan and cook over low heat until it is warm. Add the chocolates and cook until they are completely dissolved, about 3 minutes. Place the cream and chocolate mixture in a food processor fitted with a steel

continued on next page

MENU
SIX

Chocolate Bread Pudding Drizzled with Heavy Cream (*cont.*)

blade and blend. While the machine is running, gradually add the sugar, egg yolks, butter and vanilla and process until smooth. Pour the mixture over the bread cubes.

Place the egg whites and salt in an electric mixer fitted with a whisk and beat until they form stiff peaks. Gradually fold in the whites, by hand, to the chocolate mixture, and gently combine until incorporated.

Transfer to the prepared baking dish and place in a larger roasting pan filled with 2 inches of water. The baking dish should be surrounded by a bath of hot water. Transfer the roasting pan to the oven and bake until the pudding just begins to set, about 35 minutes.

Serve warm in individual bowls or cups, drizzled with the remaining ½ cup cream.

Menu Seven

Saffron Risotto with Pan-Broiled Fennel Shrimp

Pan-Broiled Zucchini

Bibb Lettuce with Red Onion and Balsamic Vinaigrette

Italian Bread

Fresh Raspberry Tart with Lemon Curd

I first ate risotto during my honeymoon at a small restaurant near a hotel we happened upon somewhere on the Italian coast. We had the classic dish, Risotto alla Milanese (risotto with saffron). The shrimp was served separately, but I liked the combination of flavors so I combined them in one dish. The dessert is not the least bit authentic, but it's one of my favorites.

TIME TIPS:

THE TART DOUGH CAN BE MADE UP TO 1 WEEK IN ADVANCE.

THE SALAD DRESSING CAN BE MADE UP TO 3 DAYS IN ADVANCE.

THE TART CAN BE MADE UP TO 4 HOURS IN ADVANCE.

THE SHRIMP CAN BE MARINATED UP TO 2 HOURS IN ADVANCE.

SAFFRON RISOTTO WITH PAN-BROILED FENNEL SHRIMP

"When you are making a risotto you should be in perfect harmony with yourself. You shouldn't be nervous or angry. It's a ritual that is going to give you so much pleasure later that it's worth spending fifteen or twenty minutes over a hot stove stirring very slowly.... It's the dish of romance. If you rush it, it's never good." (Pino Luongo, *A Tuscan in the Kitchen*, Potter, 1988)

I couldn't agree more, although I have found that risotto is so easy and so foolproof to make, it still comes out even if you're not in perfect harmony with yourself (and who ever is?). At first glance this appears to be a long list of ingredients, but most will be on hand, particularly if you've bought the essential ingredients on page 21. If you have not attempted to make risotto you will be pleasantly surprised at how easy and quick a dish this is to master.

The Ancient Greeks thought that fennel was a symbol of victory and success. The Romans thought it sharpened eyesight, but I think it's just a wonderful vegetable: mild, sweet and licorice–like in flavor, crunchy and re-freshing in texture.

For the Fennel Shrimp:
2 teaspoons olive oil
1 tablespoon Sambuca or Pernod
1 teaspoon fennel seed
2½ pounds medium-size shrimp, peeled and butterflied
½ teaspoon kosher salt
½ teaspoon black pepper

For the Saffron Risotto:

1 tablespoon olive oil

1 large Spanish onion, cut into small dice

2 carrots, peeled, if desired, and cut into small dice

1 celery stalk, cut into small dice

2½ cups arborio rice

1 teaspoon saffron threads

2 fresh or canned tomatoes, diced

1 cup white wine

9 cups chicken broth

1 tablespoon unsalted butter (optional)

½ cup freshly grated Parmesan cheese

¼ cup chopped fresh Italian flat-leaf parsley leaves, for garnish

To marinate the shrimp: Place the oil, Sambuca, fennel and shrimp in a large mixing bowl and set aside.

To make the risotto: Place a large skillet over medium heat and when it is hot, add the oil. Add the onion, carrots and celery and cook until they are soft, about 3 to 5 minutes. Add the rice and cook, stirring for 1 minute, until it is well coated. Add the saffron and tomatoes and cook for 1 minute. Add the wine and cook until it has been absorbed, about 2 minutes.

Add ½ cup broth, stirring constantly until the liquid has been absorbed by the rice.

Continue adding broth, ½ cup at a time, and cook until all the liquid has been absorbed, about 18 to 20 minutes, stirring well after each addi-

continued on next page

MENU
SEVEN

Saffron Risotto with Pan–Broiled Fennel Shrimp (*cont.*)

tion. Do not add more than 8 cups broth. Add the butter and Parmesan cheese and stir well.

Place the remaining 1 cup broth in a small saucepan and bring to a boil over high heat.

To make the Fennel Shrimp: Remove the shrimp from the marinade, discarding the excess, and sprinkle it with the salt and pepper. Place a large skillet over medium–high heat and when it is hot, add the shrimp and cook until it turns pink, about 3 minutes.

Just prior to serving, add the boiling broth to the risotto and stir well. Transfer to heated individual shallow bowls and serve immediately. Garnish with the parsley and Fennel Shrimp.

Pan-Broiled Zucchini

Although the risotto dish needs little accompaniment, I have a particular fondness for zucchini cooked this way.

> 1 tablespoon unsalted butter
> 2 garlic cloves, minced or chopped
> 3 large zucchini, trimmed and cut into coinlike slices
> 1 teaspoon kosher salt
> ½ teaspoon black pepper

Place a large skillet over medium-high heat and when it is hot, add the butter. Add the garlic and cook for 1 minute. Add the zucchini, salt and pepper and cook until the zucchini is well browned, about 4 to 5 minutes on each side. Transfer to a heated serving bowl and serve immediately.

MENU
SEVEN

Bibb Lettuce with Red Onion and Balsamic Vinaigrette

*A*lthough I am a die–hard fan of romaine lettuce, I sometimes love a salad of soft, buttery Bibb lettuce.

For the Red Onion and Balsamic Vinaigrette:
1–2 tablespoons finely chopped red onion
1 tablespoon balsamic vinegar
1 tablespoon olive oil

2–3 heads Bibb lettuce, outer leaves discarded
1 teaspoon kosher salt
2 tablespoons chopped fresh chives

To make the Red Onion and Balsamic Vinaigrette: Place the onion, balsamic vinegar and oil in a small mixing bowl and combine well.

Place the lettuce in a large salad bowl. Toss the lettuce with the dressing, sprinkle with the salt and chives and serve immediately.

Fresh Raspberry Tart with Lemon Curd

*T*art and buttery and just perfect. You can substitute blueberries, black–berries or strawberries for the raspberries or use a combination of all four.

For the Crust:

¼ cup sugar

1¼ cups pastry flour

¼ teaspoon kosher salt

5 tablespoons unsalted butter, chilled and sliced

1 small egg

For the Lemon Curd:

2 large eggs

½ cup sugar

6 tablespoons fresh lemon juice

grated zest of 1 lemon

1 cup heavy cream

4 cups fresh raspberries

To prepare the crust: Place the sugar, flour and salt in the bowl of a food processor fitted with a steel blade and pulse to combine. Add the butter, one slice at a time, and pulse until the dough resembles coarse cornmeal. Add the egg and pulse until it forms a ball. Pat it down to form a disk, cover with plastic wrap and refrigerate at least 1 hour and up to 1 week.

Preheat the oven to 350 degrees. Place a medium–size mixing bowl in the freezer.

continued on next page

MENU
SEVEN

Fresh Raspberry Tart with Lemon Curd (*cont.*)

To roll out: Place the disk on a floured surface and roll out as thinly as you can without breaking the dough. Place the dough in a 9-inch tart or pie pan. Place aluminum foil right on top of the crust and weight it down with the beans. Place in the oven 10 minutes. Remove the foil and beans and continue baking until golden, about 15 minutes. Set aside to cool.

To make the lemon curd: Place the eggs and sugar in the top of a double boiler over medium-high heat and cook until it is thick and lemon-colored, about 3 to 5 minutes. Add the lemon juice and zest and cook for 1 minute. Set aside to cool.

Place the cream in the chilled bowl and whip until it forms stiff peaks. Gently fold the cooled lemon curd into the whipped cream. Place in the cooled shell and top with the raspberries. Serve immediately or cover and refrigerate up to 4 hours.

MENU EIGHT

CHICKEN CURRY WITH COCONUT, BASIL AND MANGOES

BASMATI RICE WITH TOASTED PISTACHIO NUTS

STEAMED GREEN BEANS

ROTI, NAN OR CHAPATI

VANILLA ICE CREAM WITH BANANAS AND CARAMEL SAUCE

Although a purist would insist that you make your own curry for this Indian inspired dinner, I am very happy with the curry powders I have purchased. Roti, Nan and Chapati can be purchased at an Indian market or restaurant, or, if one is not near you, substitute warmed pita bread.

TIME TIPS:

THE CHICKEN CURRY CAN BE MADE UP TO 1 DAY AHEAD AND GENTLY REHEATED THE DAY OF THE PARTY.

MAKE THE CARAMEL SAUCE 1 DAY AHEAD.

CHICKEN CURRY WITH COCONUT, BASIL AND MANGOES

*B*efore settling on this version of Chicken Curry, I tried many different ones, but I like this one because it combines the fire of the curry with the sweetness of the mango and tomato. If your budget permits, you can sub-stitute shrimp for some or all of the chicken.

¼ cup all-purpose flour

2 tablespoons curry powder

1 teaspoon kosher salt

¼ teaspoon cayenne pepper (optional)

2½–3 pounds boneless, skinless chicken breasts, cut into large pieces

1–2 tablespoons canola oil

1 large Spanish onion, chopped

1 red bell pepper, seeded and diced

2 garlic cloves, chopped

1 tablespoon minced fresh gingerroot

4–4½ cups chicken broth

¼ cup currants, raisins, chopped dried figs or apricots

2 beefsteak tomatoes, diced

1 peach or mango, pitted and diced

1 tablespoon fresh lime juice

3 tablespoons fresh chopped cilantro leaves, for garnish

3 tablespoons fresh chopped basil leaves, for garnish

3 tablespoons shredded toasted or raw coconut, for garnish (see page 60)

Place the flour, curry powder, salt and cayenne pepper, if desired, in a bowl, mix to combine, add the chicken and toss until the chicken is dusted with the mixture.

Place a large skillet over medium–high heat and when it is hot, add the oil. Add the chicken, skin side down, one piece at a time, allowing the pan to reheat for about 30 seconds between additions. Cook until they are well browned, about 3 minutes on each side. Set aside.

Reheat the skillet and add the onion, pepper, garlic and ginger. Cook until the onion is golden, about 4 minutes. Return the chicken to the skillet, lower the heat to low and add the broth. Cook until the chicken is tender and the liquid has reduced by one–quarter.

Add the currants, tomatoes and peach and cook until they are heated through, about 3 to 5 minutes. Off heat, add the lime juice. Transfer to a heated serving platter and serve immediately. Garnish with the cilantro, basil and coconut.

MENU
EIGHT

Basmati Rice with Toasted Pistachio Nuts

2 teaspoons olive oil
½ Spanish onion, chopped
1 garlic clove, finely chopped
1½ cups basmati rice
2½ cups chicken or vegetable broth
⅓ cup toasted pistachio nuts, coarsely chopped (see note)

Place a small saucepan over medium heat and when it is hot, add the oil. Add the onion and garlic and cook until the onion is soft, about 10 minutes.

Add the rice and broth and bring to a boil. Cover, lower the heat to low and cook until the broth has been absorbed, about 20 minutes.

Add the nuts, and transfer to a heated medium size bowl. Serve immediately.

NOTE: To toast nuts: Place a heavy bottomed skillet over medium-high heat and when it is hot add the nuts. Cook, stirring constantly, until the nuts are lightly browned, about 3 to 5 minutes. Let cool.

Vanilla Ice Cream with Bananas and Caramel Sauce

*M*mm. Sweet and gooey.

You can substitute cinnamon, ginger (see page 143) or cardamom ice cream. Or, if you can't find them, let vanilla ice cream sit at room temperature for about 10 minutes and then mix in anywhere from 1 teaspoon to 1 tablespoon ground cinnamon or cardamom or a combination of both.

> *2 cups heavy cream*
> *½ cup sugar*
> *1 tablespoon unsalted butter, at room temperature*
> *6 cups vanilla ice cream*
> *2 ripe bananas, thinly sliced*

Place the cream in small pot over high heat and cook until it is just scalded. Place the sugar in another pot and cook, stirring, until it caramelizes, about 5 minutes. Add the sugar to the cream and mix until smooth. Add the butter.

Place the ice cream in individual bowls or wine glasses, top with the banana slices and drizzle with the warm caramel sauce. If necessary, you can reheat the sauce by placing it in a larger pan and warming over a very low heat.

MENU
EIGHT

BEEF CARBONNADE

PARSNIP MASHED POTATOES

FRENCH BREAD

BRUSSELS SPROUTS LEAVES WITH BROWN BUTTER

DAIN'S GRANDMOTHER'S CARROT CAKE

TIME TIPS:

MAKE THE BEEF CARBONNADE 1 TO 2 DAYS AHEAD.

MAKE THE PARSNIP MASHED POTATOES UP TO 6 HOURS AHEAD AND GENTLY REHEAT. ADD THE CREAM JUST BEFORE SERVING.

When I first met my husband, Mark, he was a salesman for Harpoon, a Boston microbrewery. Since I had a small shop that didn't sell much beer, he said, if I wanted, he would hand deliver two cases at a time. That's exactly what I wanted. I wanted lots of two-case deliveries because I wanted to see him as much as possible. Whenever I went to someone's house for dinner I brought a six-pack or two, claiming that I wanted to share this wonderful beer. The truth is that I just wanted to get rid of it, so that he would come back.

During this time, my friend Sharon Smith returned from a trip to Belgium and told me about Beef Carbonnade, a wonderfully comforting winter Belgian beef stew made with dark beer. I replaced the dark beer with Harpoon ale and discovered a newfound fondness for the combination of beer and beef. And, in the process, used up some of my reserves, causing Mark to return a little sooner.

If the Parsnip Mashed Potatoes don't appeal to you, serve egg noodles instead.

If your budget allows, serve sherry or port after dinner.

BEEF CARBONNADE

When I first made Beef Carbonnade, I included parsnips and potatoes in the stew, but now prefer having them as a separate accompaniment.

It is very important that you dry the meat well or it will not brown properly.

> *1 teaspoon kosher salt*
> *1 teaspoon black pepper*
> *¼ cup all-purpose flour*
> *3–3½ pounds beef stew meat, cut into 1–1½-inch cubes, dried with a*
> *   paper towel*
> *3 tablespoons unsalted butter*
> *2 large Spanish onions, diced*
> *5 carrots, peeled, if desired, and cut into large chunks*
> *2 celery stalks, cut into large chunks*
> *1 teaspoon dried thyme (not powdered)*
> *2 bay leaves*
> *2 bottles dark beer*
> *2 teaspoons Dijon mustard*
> *1 teaspoon fresh thyme leaves, for garnish*
> *¼ cup fresh Italian flat-leaf parsley leaves, for garnish*

Place the salt, pepper and flour on a baking sheet, mix to combine and add the beef. Toss until the beef is dusted with the mixture.

Place a large skillet over medium–high heat and when it is hot, add 2 tablespoons butter. Add the beef cubes, a few at a time, allowing the pan to reheat for about 30 seconds between additions. Cook until they are well browned on all sides, about 5 to 7 minutes. This will take two to three batches. Remove the beef cubes and set aside.

Reheat the skillet over medium heat and add the remaining 1 tablespoon butter. Add the onions and cook until caramelized, about 15 minutes. Add the carrots, celery, thyme and bay leaves and cook for 5 minutes. Return the beef to the skillet. Gradually add the beer and cook until it comes to a low simmer. Lower the heat to the lowest possible setting and cook, partially covered, for 1½ hours. Discard the bay leaves.

Cover and refrigerate overnight.

Reheat, covered, over low heat and, just prior to serving, add the mustard. Transfer to a large heated serving bowl and serve immediately. Garnish with the thyme and parsley.

MENU
NINE

Parsnip Mashed Potatoes

Native to the Mediterranean, parsnips are similar in texture to turnips and in shape to carrots; some people call parsnips white carrots. Both fruitier and nuttier than carrots, parsnips add a touch of earthiness and sweetness to traditional mashed potatoes.

If you're not up for parsnips, you can omit them and add the same weight in potatoes.

1½–2 pounds new potatoes, peeled, if desired, and diced (about 12)
½–¾ pound parsnips, peeled and sliced
1 teaspoon kosher salt
½–¾ cup heavy cream

Place the potatoes and parsnips in a large pot, cover with cold water and bring to a boil over high heat. Cook until both are very tender, about 20 to 25 minutes. Drain off the water.

Off heat and mash with a fork or potato masher, gradually incorporating the salt and cream. If necessary, reheat over a very low heat. Transfer to a medium-size heated serving bowl and serve immediately.

Brussels Sprouts Leaves with Brown Butter

*A*lthough these require more work than simply tossing Brussels sprouts into a pot of steaming water, their taste is nothing less than magnificent. Additionally, I can guarantee that if you do not say what they are, even the most ardent Brussels sprout detractor will be impressed.

Pulling the leaves apart takes some time and if you don't have or don't want to spend the time, you can shred them. Shredded leaves don't look as elegant but the dish tastes just as great. Either way they must be prepared and cooked just before eating.

> ¼ cup unsalted butter
> 6 pounds Brussels sprouts, root end trimmed, leaves pulled apart and
>   center (heart) quartered
> 1 teaspoon kosher salt
> ½ teaspoon black pepper
> ½ teaspoon grated orange zest
> ¼ cup fresh orange juice

Place the butter in a large skillet over medium–high heat and cook until it turns brown, about 3 minutes. Add the Brussels sprouts leaves and cook until they are well coated with butter and turn bright green, about 3 to 5 minutes. Add the salt, pepper, orange zest and orange juice and cook for 1 minute. Transfer to a medium–size heated serving bowl and serve immediately.

MENU
NINE

Dain's Grandmother's Carrot Cake

When I was in college I had a friend named Dain Fritz who used his truck to help me move a piece of very heavy furniture. Since I knew he loved carrot cake, I made him one as a way of saying thanks. Although he was gracious and appreciative, when the cake had been completely consumed he told me that the best carrot cake he had ever had was his grandmother's. So when it came time for his birthday I called his mother, who called her mother, who sent me the following recipe. I have never had a better carrot cake.

I make this in a bundt pan and I use half the icing called for in the recipe.

For the Cake:
1¼ cups canola or vegetable oil

2 cups sugar

4 large eggs

3 cups grated carrots

2 cups all-purpose flour

1 teaspoon kosher salt

1 teaspoon ground cinnamon

2 teaspoons baking soda

For the Cream Cheese Icing:
½ cup unsalted butter, at room temperature

8 ounces cream cheese, at room temperature

2 cups confectioners' sugar

2 teaspoons vanilla extract

1 cup toasted walnuts or pecans, chopped (see page 102)

Preheat the oven to 350 degrees. Lightly butter and flour an 8 x 13 x 3-inch pan or a bundt pan.

To make the cake: Place the oil, sugar and eggs in a mixer and blend until well incorporated. Add the carrots, flour, salt, cinnamon and baking soda and mix until well incorporated. Transfer to the prepared pan and bake for 40 minutes. Set aside to cool.

While the cake is baking, prepare the icing: Place the butter and cream cheese in a mixer and mix until well incorporated. Add the sugar and vanilla and blend. When the cake has cooled, spread with the icing. Sprinkle with the nuts and cut into 12 pieces.

MENU
NINE

Menu Ten

Roasted Chicken Breasts with Dried Figs, Apricots and Prunes

French Bread

Mixed Green Salad with Red Onions and Toasted Pine Nuts

Rice Pudding

Inspired by the Mediterranean custom of combining dried fruit in savory dishes, this entire menu can be served hot on a beautifully set dinner table, with candelabra and white linens, but it is equally fabulous cold, served on paper plates set on a blanket.

TIME TIPS:

MARINATE THE CHICKEN THE NIGHT BEFORE.

MAKE THE RICE PUDDING THE DAY BEFORE.

Roasted Chicken Breasts with Dried Figs, Apricots and Prunes

Bone-in, skin–on chicken breasts work best for this recipe.

> ***For the Marinade:***
> *3 garlic cloves, minced*
> *3 tablespoons black olive paste (available at specialty food stores)*
> *1½ teaspoons dried Greek oregano*
> *1½ teaspoons fennel seed*
> *3 bay leaves*
> *⅓ cup white wine*
> *3 tablespoons red wine vinegar*
> *2 tablespoons olive oil*
> *6 dried figs*
> *12 dried apricots*
> *12 prunes*
> *⅓–½ cup capers, rinsed*
> *1 cup kalamata olives*
>
> *6 chicken breasts, trimmed of excess fat*
> *1 teaspoon kosher salt*
> *½ teaspoon black pepper*
> *1 tablespoon olive or canola oil*
> *3 tablespoons light brown sugar*

Place the marinade ingredients in a large nonreactive glass or ceramic bowl, add the chicken, cover and refrigerate overnight.

Preheat the oven to 350 degrees.

Remove the chicken pieces and dry them with a paper towel. Place the marinade in a small pot and bring to a boil over high heat. Cook 3 minutes and set aside. Sprinkle the chicken with the salt and pepper. Place a large skillet over medium–high heat and when it is hot, add the oil. Add the chicken pieces, one at a time, allowing the pan to reheat for about 30 seconds between additions. Cook until they are browned, about 5 minutes on each side.

Transfer the chicken to a large baking pan, sprinkle with the brown sugar, add the reserved marinade and place in the oven. Bake until the chicken is cooked throughout, about 20 minutes. Remove the bay leaves. Transfer to a large heated serving platter and serve immediately.

MENU
TEN

Mixed Green Salad with Red Onions and Toasted Pine Nuts

1 head red leaf lettuce, torn
1 head green leaf lettuce, torn
½ red onion, thinly sliced
¼ cup toasted pine nuts (see page 102)
3 tablespoons extra-virgin olive oil
3 tablespoons red wine vinegar
1 teaspoon kosher salt
½ teaspoon black pepper

Place the lettuces, onion and pine nuts in a large salad bowl. Drizzle with the oil and vinegar and sprinkle with the salt and pepper. Serve immediately.

Rice Pudding

After the complex flavor of the roasted chicken breasts, this comforting and simple rice pudding is a welcome change for dessert. Use whole or 2% milk for the best texture and taste. Serve it with strong Greek coffee or espresso.

> *2 teaspoons unsalted butter*
> *1¼ cups arborio rice*
> *pinch kosher salt*
> *2 cups water*
> *3 cups milk*
> *¼ cup sugar*
> *2 large egg yolks*
> *1 teaspoon vanilla extract*
> *⅛–¼ teaspoon ground cinnamon*
> *½ cup heavy cream*
> *¼–⅓ cup finely chopped toasted walnuts or pecans, for garnish*
>   *(optional) (see page 102)*

Place a medium–size heavy-bottomed saucepan over medium heat and add the butter. When the butter has melted, add the rice and salt, stirring constantly until the rice is well coated with the butter. Add ¼ cup water, stirring constantly until it has been absorbed by the rice. Continue adding the water and then the milk, ½ cup at a time, and cook, stirring occasionally, until the rice is al dente, about 20 to 25 minutes. It should be runny.

Place the sugar, egg yolks, vanilla and cinnamon in a small mixing bowl and mix well.

Add the egg mixture to the rice and stir vigorously with a wooden

continued on next page

MENU
TEN

Rice Pudding (*cont.*)

spoon until it is well incorporated. Cook for 2 minutes. Set aside to cool to room temperature.

Place the cream in a small copper or metal bowl and place in the freezer for 5 minutes. Beat with a whisk until it forms soft peaks. Gently fold into the rice pudding. When it has cooled to room temperature, transfer to individual serving bowls or wine glasses. Serve immediately or cover and refrigerate at least 1 and up to 8 hours. Garnish with the walnuts, if desired.

MENU ELEVEN

Fresh Asparagus Salad

French Bread

Wild Mushroom Risotto with Radicchio Salad

Pecan Butter Cookies and Fresh Berries

Although I should know better, when my vegetarian friend Beth Wolfensberger came to dinner with her meat–eating husband, David Singer, I was stymied. In addition, Beth was hugely pregnant and I felt that I had to serve something substantial. Risotto seemed a perfect choice. While I had combined mushrooms and asparagus in risotto before I wanted to pair them in the meal but not in one dish. Although the asparagus can be served at any point in the meal, I wanted something leafy and the risotto needed some color; hence, the radicchio garnish. I have made this meal many times since; it's ample, comforting and satisfying to meat eaters and vegetarians alike. See page 224 for the recipe for the Pecan Butter Cookies.

TIME TIPS:

MAKE THE ASPARAGUS SALAD UP TO 4 HOURS AHEAD OF TIME.

THE COOKIES CAN BE MADE 2 DAYS AHEAD.

Fresh Asparagus Salad

*T*his salad can be eaten hot or cold, as a starter, with the risotto or after. For a more dramatic presentation, you can use half green asparagus and half white, which, while more tender, is a bit less flavorful—and more expensive.

If you don't like black olives, omit the black olive paste.

> *3 bunches asparagus, trimmed, and if thick, peeled*
> *3 tablespoons extra-virgin olive oil*
> *3 tablespoon fresh lemon or orange juice*
> *1 tablespoon black olive paste*
> *½ teaspoon kosher salt*
> *½ teaspoon black pepper*
> *1 shallot, minced*

Fill a large bowl with ice water.

Bring a large pot of water to a boil over high heat. Add the asparagus and cook until it is bright green, about 2 to 3 minutes. Drain, place in the ice water and drain again. Transfer to a large shallow serving bowl and add the oil, lemon juice, olive paste, salt, pepper and shallot. Toss lightly. Serve immediately or cover and refrigerate up to 4 hours.

Wild Mushroom Risotto with Radicchio Salad

Egyptian pharaohs forbade their subjects to eat mushrooms because they considered them to be the food of the gods and saved them for themselves, but I see no reason not to share this luxurious risotto with your guests.

The best time to clean mushrooms is just before you use them. Use a soft brush (you can buy a special one for mushrooms) or a slightly damp towel. Never soak them.

If you want to get really fancy (and go over your $50 limit), drizzle a little white truffle oil on each plate.

> 2 tablespoons unsalted butter
>
> 3 large leeks, well washed, white part only, cut into very small dice
>
> 3 cups fresh shiitake, chanterelle or portobello mushrooms, or a combination, trimmed and chopped
>
> 3 cups arborio rice
>
> ¾ cup white wine
>
> 10 cups chicken or mushroom broth or a combination
>
> 1 tablespoon fresh lemon juice
>
> 1 small head radicchio, minced
>
> 3 scallion greens, minced
>
> ¼ tomato, minced
>
> 1 teaspoon finely chopped rosemary leaves
>
> 1 tablespoon finely chopped fresh marjoram, rosemary or basil leaves or chives or a combination
>
> ¼ cup heavy cream (optional)
>
> ¾–1 cup freshly grated Parmesan cheese

continued on next page

MENU
ELEVEN

Wild Mushroom Risotto with Radicchio Salad (*cont.*)

Place a large skillet over medium heat and when it is hot, add 1 tablespoon butter. Add the leeks and mushrooms and cook until they are soft, about 3 to 5 minutes. Add the rice and cook, stirring, for 1 minute, until it is well coated. Add the wine and cook until it has been absorbed, about 2 minutes.

Add ½ cup of the broth, stirring constantly until the liquid has been absorbed by the rice.

Continue adding the broth, ½ cup at a time, and cook until all the liquid has been absorbed, about 18 to 20 minutes, stirring well after each addition. Do not add more than 9 cups of broth. Add the remaining 1 tablespoon butter, if desired, and stir well. Place the remaining 1 cup broth in a small saucepan and bring to a boil.

While the risotto is cooking, place the lemon juice, radicchio, scallion greens, tomato and rosemary in a small mixing bowl, mix and set aside.

Just prior to serving, add the boiling broth to the risotto, stir well and add the fresh herbs, the cream, if desired, and Parmesan cheese. Divide between 6 heated individual shallow bowls and top with equal amounts of the radicchio mixture. Serve immediately.

AVGOLEMONO SOUP

EGGPLANT AND LAMB MOUSSAKA

MIXED GREENS WITH PISTACHIO–LEMON DRESSING

FRESH FIGS, RED GRAPES AND PECAN BUTTER COOKIES

When I was in college I traveled to Greece and ate so much moussaka I thought I'd never want to eat it again when I returned to the States. Not so: as soon as I got back, I started searching cookbooks and playing with recipes until I found one that resembled what I had had in Greece—with a twist of my own.

TIME TIPS:

ASSEMBLE THE EGGPLANT AND LAMB MOUSSAKA 2 DAYS AHEAD.

PREPARE THE PISTACHIO–LEMON DRESSING 2 DAYS AHEAD.

BAKE THE EGGPLANT AND LAMB MOUSSAKA 1 DAY AHEAD.

MAKE THE AVGOLEMONO UP TO 2 DAYS AHEAD.

PECAN BUTTER cookies CAN BE MADE UP TO 2 DAYS AHEAD.

Avgolemono Soup

*T*here's nothing easier, cheaper or more soothing than this Greek egg lemon soup.

> *12 cups homemade chicken broth or low-sodium canned*
> *½–⅔ cup orzo or rice*
> *12 large egg yolks*
> *⅓–½ cup fresh lemon juice*
> *¼ cup chopped fresh Italian flat-leaf parsley or dill leaves*

Place the chicken broth in a large stockpot and bring to a boil over high heat. Add the orzo, lower the heat to low and cook until it is tender, about 15 minutes.

While the orzo is cooking, place the egg yolks and lemon juice in a bowl and whisk until the mixture is frothy and somewhat thickened.

Gradually add ½ cup boiling broth to the egg mixture, being careful not to let the eggs curdle. Add 2 more cups, ½ cup at a time. Return the mixture to the stock pot and continue cooking for 10 minutes, whisking occasionally. Serve immediately or cover and refrigerate up to 2 days.

To reheat, cook over low heat until heated through, about 5 to 8 minutes. Garnish with the parsley or dill.

Eggplant and Lamb Moussaka

*L*ike lasagna, moussaka is best made two days before your party and then refrigerated overnight. The night before, bake and refrigerate it, then reheat it when your guests arrive. I like to serve moussaka straight from the baking pan.

If you are a vegetarian, omit the lamb and double the tomatoes.

For the Tomato Sauce:

1 tablespoon olive oil

1 large Spanish onion, chopped

3 garlic cloves, chopped

1 pound ground lamb

¼ cup white wine

2 cups fresh or canned diced tomatoes, partially drained of juice

2 tablespoons tomato paste

2 bay leaves

1 teaspoon ground cinnamon

pinch ground nutmeg

2 teaspoons dried Greek oregano

2 tablespoons chopped fresh Italian flat-leaf parsley leaves

For the Béchamel Sauce:

½ cup unsalted butter

½ cup all-purpose flour

5 cups milk

pinch ground nutmeg

pinch white pepper

½ teaspoon kosher salt

continued on next page

MENU
TWELVE

Eggplant and Lamb Moussaka (*cont.*)

For the Eggplant Layer:
2 pounds eggplant, peeled and thinly sliced
1 tablespoon olive oil
1 teaspoon kosher salt
½ teaspoon black pepper

½ cup finely chopped or coarsely ground, toasted bread crumbs
½ cup freshly grated Parmesan cheese

Preheat the oven to 350 degrees. Butter a 9 x 12-inch pan.

To make the tomato sauce: Place a large skillet over medium heat and when it is hot, add the oil. Add the onion and garlic and cook until golden, about 3 minutes.

Add the lamb, breaking it up with the back of a wooden spoon, and cook until it loses its rawness, about 7 to 10 minutes. Add the wine and cook until it has been absorbed, about 3 minutes. Lower the heat to low, add the tomatoes, tomato paste, bay leaves, cinnamon, nutmeg, oregano and cook until it begins to thicken, about 1 hour. Remove the bay leaves, add the parsley and set aside.

To make the béchamel sauce: Place the butter in a large skillet and when it has melted, gradually whisk in the flour. Cook until it has the consistency of mashed potatoes. Gradually add the milk, whisking all the while and cook until smooth, about 5 to 7 minutes. Add the nutmeg, pepper and salt. Set aside.

Preheat the oven to 400 degrees. While the sauce is cooking, prepare the eggplant.

Toss the eggplants with the oil, salt and pepper and place on a baking sheet. Bake until golden, about 15 minutes.

Place the bread crumbs and Parmesan cheese in a small mixing bowl and toss to combine.

To assemble the moussaka: Sprinkle the bottom of the prepared pan with ⅓ of the bread crumb mixture, ⅓ of the eggplant slices and ½ of the tomato sauce. Sprinkle again with ⅓ of the bread crumb mixture, ⅓ of the eggplant slices and the remaining tomato sauce. Top with the remaining ⅓ eggplant slices and the bechamel sauce. Sprinkle with the remaining bread crumb mixture. Cover with plastic wrap and press down, allowing the layers to tighten up. Cover and refrigerate.

Preheat the oven to 350 degrees.

Remove the plastic wrap and transfer the moussaka to the oven. Bake until lightly browned, about 40 to 50 minutes. Let cool for 20 minutes, cover with aluminum foil and refrigerate overnight.

To reheat: Preheat the oven to 350 degrees. Do not remove the foil. Place the moussaka in the oven and bake until hot, about 30 minutes. Serve immediately.

MENU
TWELVE

MIXED GREENS WITH
PISTACHIO-LEMON DRESSING

*A*lthough this dressing is perfectly suited to this meal, it can be used on any green salad.

> *6 tablespoons coarsely chopped pistachio nuts*
> *1 tablespoon walnut oil*
> *3 tablespoons olive or canola oil*
> *¼ cup fresh lemon juice*
> *1 large head Bibb lettuce, outer leaves discarded, inner leaves washed*
> *   and torn*
> *1 large head radicchio, torn apart*
> *1 teaspoon kosher salt*
> *½ teaspoon black pepper*

To make the Pistachio-Lemon dressing: Place 3 tablespoons of the pistachio nuts, the oils and lemon juice in a blender and blend until creamy.

Place the Bibb lettuce and radicchio in a large salad bowl and toss with the dressing. Sprinkle with the salt, pepper and remaining 3 tablespoons pistachio nuts. Serve immediately.

Fresh Figs, Red Grapes
and Pecan Butter Cookies

Serve with strong Greek coffee or mint tea.

Although many people are fond of warm cookies, I think that the Pecan Butter Cookies (see page 224) are best served hours, if not a day or two after they're made. As they are very rich, allow two to three per person and serve them on individual plates with one fresh fig, quartered through the root end, and a small bunch of red or purple grapes.

Menu
Twelve

About four years ago, I wrote a story about taking three Boston chefs to three unsuspecting households to cook a three-course meal with whatever they could find in the pantry, refrigerator and freezer. Susan Regis, the chef at Biba, was paired with Carol and Maury Sapoznik, whose cupboards resembled the shelves of a very well-stocked, high quality gourmet food shop. Carol, the regional manager of Crate and Barrel, and Maury, the principal of Brookline High School, are talented and avid cooks with a pantry full of exceptional equipment. Susan had a blast. This meal is my re-creation of her menu.

TIME TIPS:

ASSEMBLE BUT DO NOT COOK THE CHICKEN SALTIMBOCCA UP TO 4 HOURS AHEAD.

ASSEMBLE BUT DO NOT COOK THE ROASTED BUTTERNUT SQUASH UP TO 4 HOURS AHEAD.

MAKE THE ANCHOVY DRESSING THE DAY BEFORE.

Chicken Saltimbocca with Panfried Sage Leaves

Saltimbocca means to "jump into the mouth." This version of the classic Italian veal dish certainly does.

Note: Do not substitute dried sage leaves! If you can't find fresh, skip this recipe.

3 whole skinless, boneless chicken breasts, halved, excess fat removed
2 tablespoons olive oil
6 garlic cloves, thinly sliced
16–20 fresh sage leaves
4–6 thin slices prosciutto (optional)
¼–⅓ cup freshly shaved Parmesan cheese
1 tablespoon all-purpose flour
1 teaspoon kosher salt
½ cup white wine

Flatten each breast by pounding it between two pieces of waxed paper with a mallet, rolling pin or bottle. Pound it as thin as possible, being careful not to tear the chicken. Set aside.

Place a large nonstick or cast-iron skillet over medium heat and when it is hot, add 1 tablespoon oil. Add the garlic and sage and cook until both are lightly toasted, about 2 minutes. Set the pan aside but do not wash it.

Place half a slice of prosciutto, if desired, and about 1 tablespoon of the Parmesan cheese inside each chicken breast. Top with equal amounts of half of the reserved garlic and sage. Fold each chicken breast and seal the edges by pinching with your fingers. Dust each chicken breast with flour and salt.

Reheat the skillet and, if necessary, add the remaining 1 tablespoon oil to the pan. Add the chicken breasts, skin side down, one at a time, allowing the pan to reheat for about 30 seconds between additions. Cook about 4 minutes on the first side and 3 minutes on the second. Transfer the chicken to 6 heated individual plates.

Raise the heat to high, add the wine and bring to a boil. Cook until it is reduced by half, about 2 minutes. Pour over the chicken and garnish with the remaining half of the reserved garlic and sage. Serve immediately.

MENU
THIRTEEN

Roasted Butternut Squash and Granny Smith Apples with Walnuts and Currants

Susan made butternut squash and apples in filo dough and it was superb. Although I am a fan of eating filo, I am not a fan of cooking with it. The recipe has been simplified but the flavors remain the same.

1 large butternut squash, peeled, seeded and cut into large dice
2 Granny Smith apples, peeled and cut into large dice
¼ cup coarsely chopped walnuts
2 tablespoons melted, unsalted butter
1 teaspoon kosher salt
½ teaspoon black pepper
¼ cup currants, for garnish

Preheat the oven to 400 degrees.

Place the squash, apples, walnuts, butter, salt and pepper in a large baking pan and toss to combine. Transfer the pan to the oven and bake until the squash is tender and brown, about 40 minutes. Serve immediately and garnish with the currants.

Romaine Salad with Anchovy Dressing

*V*ery similar to Caesar salad dressing but packed with even more anchovy flavor. Definitely not for the meek.

For the Dressing:
4 garlic cloves
3 anchovy fillets
½ teaspoon Dijon mustard
¼ cup fresh lemon juice
¼ cup olive oil

2 heads romaine lettuce, pale green inner leaves only, torn
1 teaspoon kosher salt
½ teaspoon black pepper

To make the anchovy dressing: Place the garlic, anchovies, mustard and lemon juice in a blender and blend until thoroughly combined. While the machine is running, gradually add the oil.

Place the lettuce in a large serving bowl, add the dressing and sprinkle with the salt and pepper. Toss gently and serve immediately.

MENU
THIRTEEN

TRIO OF SORBETS AND COOKIE PLATTER

*P*ick three of your favorite fruit sorbets and place one small scoop of each in wine glasses. Garnish with fresh mint leaves. Pass a plate of assorted cookies.

Menu Fourteen

Cashew Noodles with Asparagus and Peppers
Glazed Baby Back Ribs
Asian Slaw
Ginger Ice Cream with Bittersweet Chocolate Sauce

Unless you cook Asian food on a regular basis, you probably won't have a number of the ingredients on hand. If you have to buy them for this menu, it will bump your cost over $50 initially. The good news is they keep indefinitely, and can be used to kick up your everyday cooking. All are available at Asian specialty food stores and any well-stocked grocery store in a big city. This is a great meal for a summer barbecue.

TIME TIPS:

Prepare the Glazed Baby Back Ribs the day before.

Prepare the dressing for the Cashew Noodles up to one week ahead.

Make the Cashew Noodles up to 4 hours ahead.

Make the Asian Slaw up to 4 hours ahead.

Mix the candied ginger with the vanilla ice cream up to 1 week ahead.

Cashew Noodles with Asparagus and Peppers

This is a great dish to make in the summer when you can barely stand to be in the kitchen. The only cooking required is that you boil water, and even the hottest kitchen can tolerate that.

Although the dressing has a lot of ingredients, once you have them on hand, it will be easy to put together. The dressing is also great on cold chicken, so consider doubling the recipe for future use. It will store well for at least one week, but should be used at room temperature.

For the Salad:

¾ pound spaghetti or rotini, cooked and cooled

1 pound thin asparagus, trimmed, blanched, shocked and cut into
    thirds

½ bunch scallions, coarsely chopped, green parts left long

1 red bell pepper, thinly sliced

½ yellow bell pepper, thinly sliced

For the Dressing:

1 cup toasted cashews (see page 102)

1 quarter-size slice fresh gingerroot, peeled, if desired

2 garlic cloves

¼ teaspoon sugar

¼ teaspoon black pepper

¼ teaspoon dry mustard

½ teaspoon chili powder

pinch cayenne pepper

½ teaspoon kosher salt

½–⅔ cup strong brewed tea

2 tablespoons soy sauce
⅓ cup rice wine vinegar
1 tablespoon toasted sesame oil
½ cup canola oil

To make the salad: Place the spaghetti, asparagus, scallions and peppers in a large mixing bowl.

To make the dressing: Place the cashews, gingerroot, garlic, sugar, pepper, mustard, chili, cayenne pepper and salt in a blender or a food processor fitted with a steel blade and process until smooth. While the machine is running, gradually add the tea, soy sauce, vinegar and oils and blend well. Pour the dressing over the salad and toss. Transfer to a large serving bowl and serve immediately.

MENU
FOUR-
TEEN

Glazed Baby Back Ribs

My friend Nancy Olin wanted to make this dish for a Memorial Day dinner but was going to be out of town until 1 P.M. on the day of the dinner. So she prepared it on the Friday before, froze it, defrosted it when she got back into town and grilled it. I was one of the guests and if she hadn't told me, I'd never have guessed.

The glaze can also be used on pork chops, country-style ribs and chicken.

For the Glaze:

2 garlic cloves, minced

1 teaspoon five-spice powder (optional)

1 teaspoon chopped fresh gingerroot

½–1 teaspoon crushed red pepper flakes

¼ cup hoisin sauce

¼ cup plum sauce

¼ cup oyster sauce

3 tablespoons soy sauce

⅓ cup sherry vinegar

3 racks baby back ribs (about 2–2½ pounds each)

1 teaspoon kosher salt

½ teaspoon black pepper

½ bunch scallion greens, chopped, for garnish

¼ cup coarsely chopped cilantro leaves, for garnish

To make the glaze: Place all the glaze ingredients in a small saucepan and bring to a boil over medium-high heat. Set aside to cool.

Preheat the oven to 250 degrees.

Place the ribs in a large baking pan and cook for 1½ hours. Drain off the fat and coat with the glaze. Cover and refrigerate overnight.

To cook the ribs: Prepare a grill or preheat the broiler.

Place the ribs on the grill or on a large baking sheet, sprinkle with the salt and pepper and cook until deeply browned, about 10 to 15 minutes. Cut into 6 slabs, transfer to a heated platter and serve immediately. Garnish with the scallions and cilantro.

MENU FOUR-TEEN

Asian Slaw

*T*his crunchy, colorful slaw is a delicious change from the mayonnaise-laden American version.

For the Dressing:
6 tablespoons seasoned rice wine vinegar
6 tablespoons canola oil
1 tablespoon sugar
1 teaspoon black pepper
1 teaspoon kosher salt

1 head red cabbage, shredded
2 carrots, peeled, if desired, and cut into julienne
8 scallions, finely sliced

¼ cup lightly toasted sliced almonds, for garnish (see page 102)
¼ cup lightly toasted sesame seeds, for garnish (see page 102)

To make the dressing: Place the vinegar, oil, sugar, pepper and salt in a blender or bowl and mix to combine.

Place the cabbage, carrots and scallions in a medium-size serving bowl and toss. Add the dressing and toss to combine. Cover and refrigerate up to 4 hours or serve immediately. Garnish with the almonds and sesame seeds.

Ginger Ice Cream with Bittersweet Chocolate Sauce

I live near (perhaps too near) an ice cream shop called Rancatore's that serves the best ginger ice cream in the world. It's so ginger-y it almost hurts. If you aren't fortunate enough to live near Rancatore's or can't find ginger ice cream near where you live, try adding chopped candied ginger to vanilla ice cream. It's fabulous solo, but the Bittersweet Chocolate Sauce (see page 190) is a great addition.

MENU
FOUR-
TEEN

MENU FIFTEEN

Prosciutto-Wrapped Mango Slices
Pasta Alfredo with Broccoli Rabe
Crusty Italian Bread
Hazelnut Torte with Chocolate Glaze

I consider a dish especially successful when the people eating it enjoy food they don't normally like. The first time I made Pasta Alfredo with Broccoli Rabe was just for my husband, Mark, and myself. I served it alone—main dish and vegetable in one. Although I am not fond of Pasta Alfredo, I loved this dish, because the broccoli rabe cut the richness and intensity of the heavy cream (which was what I didn't like). Mark, on the other hand, is not fond of broccoli rabe but loved the dish because the Alfredo sauce cut the bitterness of the vegetable (which was what he didn't like).

If you want to get a little fancier or if you feel you need a salad, go really simple: mesclun greens or butter lettuce laced with salt, pepper and a mustard-y flavored vinaigrette.

TIME TIPS:

MAKE THE PROSCIUTTO-WRAPPED MANGO SLICES UP TO 4 HOURS AHEAD.

MAKE THE HAZELNUT TORTE THE DAY BEFORE.

PROSCIUTTO-WRAPPED MANGO SLICES

Salty and sweet followed by creamy and bitter. Ahhh . . .

You can substitute papaya, fresh figs or any kind of melon for the mango. Or try breadsticks.

> *2 mangoes, each cut into 6 wedges*
> *12 thin slices prosciutto*
> *½ teaspoon black pepper*
> *1 orange or lime, cut into 6 wedges*

Wrap each mango wedge with a prosciutto slice and sprinkle lightly with black pepper.

Just before serving, squeeze the orange or lime juice over each slice.

Pasta Alfredo with Broccoli Rabe

This is a quick and easy pasta dish that takes no longer to make than the time it takes to boil the spaghetti. It is a perfect introduction for those who haven't tried broccoli rabe, but if you know you don't like it, substitute spinach.

1½ pounds spaghetti

1 large or 2 small bunches broccoli rabe, trimmed and coarsely chopped

1½ cups heavy cream

⅓–½ cup chicken or vegetable broth

¼ teaspoon ground nutmeg, or more to taste

1 teaspoon kosher salt

½ teaspoon black pepper

¾ cup freshly grated Parmesan cheese, plus additional for garnish

Bring a large pot of water to a boil.

Add the spaghetti and cook for 5 minutes (it will not be done). Add the broccoli rabe and cook until the pasta is al dente, about 7 minutes. Drain and place in a large mixing bowl.

When you add the broccoli rabe to the pasta, place the cream and the broth in a small saucepan and bring to a boil over a medium–high heat. Reduce the heat to medium and cook, stirring occasionally, until the mixture has reduced by half, about 5 minutes.

Add the nutmeg, salt, pepper and Parmesan cheese to the cream and stir until well blended. Pour over the spaghetti–broccoli rabe mixture and transfer to 6 heated shallow bowls. Serve immediately. Garnish with additional Parmesan cheese.

MENU
FIFTEEN

HAZELNUT TORTE WITH CHOCOLATE GLAZE

*B*oston photographer Peter Vanderwarker gave me this fabulous recipe about eighteen years ago, but I remember few of the details.

I don't know if this was supposed to be glazed on the sides, but I never did. It's a little rustic looking, which is fine with me, but if you prefer something more finished, make 1½ times the glaze and cover the sides.

For the Hazelnut Torte:
6 large egg whites
2–2½ cups toasted hazelnuts, finely ground (see page 102)
1 cup sugar

For the Chocolate Glaze:
2 tablespoons unsalted butter
4 ounces unsweetened chocolate
½ cup milk
8 tablespoons confectioners' sugar

Preheat the oven to 350 degrees. Lightly butter an 8-inch spring-form pan.

To prepare the torte: Place the egg whites in a large mixing bowl and whip until they form stiff peaks. Fold in the nuts and sugar and pour into the prepared pan. Transfer to the oven and bake until the top is golden and the sides start to pull away from the pan, about 40 to 45 minutes. Set aside to cool.

While the torte is baking, prepare the glaze: Place the butter and chocolate in a medium-size saucepan over very low heat and cook until melted. Whisk in the milk and 6 tablespoons of the confectioners' sugar and mix until fully incorporated. Set aside to cool.

Slice the torte in half and glaze both layers. Reassemble the halves. Serve immediately or cover and refrigerate for up to 24 hours. Let warm to room temperature just before serving. Dust with the remaining 2 tablespoons confectioners' sugar.

MENU
FIFTEEN

Menu Sixteen

Chilled Corn Soup with Tomatoes, Red Peppers and Cilantro

Spice-Rubbed Catfish

Polenta Triangles

Grilled Pineapple and Avocado Salad with Walnut Oil Vinaigrette

Jake and Earl's Six-Layer Bars with Chocolate, Pecans and Coconut

This menu is created from quintessentially American ingredients but not from any particular culinary tradition. A little bit of this and a little bit of that makes this one of my favorite late summer, early fall dinners.

TIME TIPS:

Make the Chilled Corn Soup the day before.

Assemble or make the Six-Layer Bars the day before. If just assembling, bake 4 hours before.

Grill the pineapple the day before.

Rub the spices on the catfish the night before.

Make but do not cook the polenta the day before.

Chilled Corn Soup with Tomatoes, Red Peppers and Cilantro

Made from the last summer corn and best summer tomatoes, this soup should be made with only the freshest ingredients. Don't be tempted to substitute canned or frozen; it won't be the same.

To remove the corn from the cob, stand it on its stem and cut from top to bottom with a very sharp knife.

1 tablespoon olive oil

1 small Spanish onion, chopped

1–2 garlic cloves, minced

8 large ears of corn, kernels scraped off (about 5–6 cups)

1 beefsteak tomato, diced

½ teaspoon black pepper

6–7 cups chicken broth

½ red bell pepper, diced, for garnish

2–3 tablespoons chopped fresh cilantro leaves, for garnish

Place a large stockpot over medium heat and when it is hot, add the oil. Add the onion and garlic and cook until they are golden, about 3 to 4 minutes. Add the corn, tomato and black pepper and cook for 5 minutes, stirring occasionally.

Raise the heat to high, add the broth and bring to a boil. Lower the heat to medium and cook for 5 minutes.

Transfer half the solids to a blender and puree. Transfer all the soup (pureed and chunky) to a bowl, cover and refrigerate at least 2 hours and up to overnight. Garnish with the red bell pepper and cilantro.

SPICE-RUBBED CATFISH

Catfish is an underused fish with a bad reputation for having little taste and little texture. But I like the way its unassuming taste and texture contrast with the spices in this dish.

For the Spice Rub:

1 tablespoon dried Greek oregano

2 teaspoons cayenne pepper

1 heaping tablespoon garlic powder

2 teaspoons dried thyme

2 teaspoons Hungarian paprika

1½ teaspoons kosher salt

1 teaspoon black pepper

six 6–8 ounce catfish fillets, about 2½–3 pounds

1 tablespoon olive oil

1½ lemons or limes, cut into 6 slices, for garnish

To make the spice rub: Place the oregano, cayenne pepper, garlic powder, thyme, paprika, salt and pepper in a small mixing bowl and combine well.

Place the catfish on a large plate and rub both sides with the spice mixture. Cover and refrigerate at least 1 hour and up to overnight.

Prepare the grill or place a large skillet over high heat. If you are grilling, lightly rub each side with the olive oil and place the fish, skin side down, on the grill and cook for about 4 to 5 minutes on each side.

continued on next page

MENU
SIXTEEN

Spice-Rubbed Catfish (*cont.*)

If you are panfrying, place a large skillet over high heat and when it is hot, add the oil. Add the fish, skin side down, one at a time, allowing the pan to reheat for about 30 seconds between additions. Cook until deeply browned and cooked throughout, about 4 to 5 minutes on each side. Transfer to a large platter and serve immediately. Garnish with the lemon.

Polenta Triangles

You can certainly serve this polenta soft, right out of the pan, but if you want to make it ahead of time, panfrying it is very simple. You can also substitute with Mashed Potatoes (see page 108) or Corn Bread (see page 162).

> *6 cups water*
> *½–1 teaspoon kosher salt*
> *1¾–2 cups stone-ground yellow cornmeal*
> *½ cup heavy cream*
> *1 tablespoon unsalted butter*
> *1 bunch scallion greens, chopped (optional)*
> *1 tablespoon olive oil*

Lightly butter a 9-inch round baking pan.

Place the water and salt in a medium-size saucepan and bring to a boil over high heat. Gradually pour in the cornmeal, whisking all the while.

When the mixture begins to bubble, reduce the heat to medium-low and cook until the cornmeal begins to thicken, about 10 to 15 minutes.

Slowly whisk in the cream, butter, and if desired, the scallions. Continue cooking until the polenta just begins to pull away from the sides of the pan.

Pour the polenta into the prepared pan, cover and refrigerate up to overnight. Just before serving, cut into 6 triangles. Place a large skillet over medium-high heat and when it is hot, add the oil. Place the triangles on the skillet and cook until browned, about 3 minutes on each side. Serve immediately.

If you want to serve the polenta soft, skip the last step and serve immediately.

MENU
SIXTEEN

GRILLED PINEAPPLE AND AVOCADO SALAD WITH WALNUT OIL VINAIGRETTE

*A*lthough this combination may be difficult to imagine, it is quite wonderful.

For the Vinaigrette:

2 teaspoons olive oil

2 teaspoons walnut oil

1 tablespoon plus 1 teaspoon red wine vinegar or lemon or orange juice

1 teaspoon kosher salt

¼–½ teaspoon black pepper

1 pineapple, cut into 12 slices

2 bunches watercress, well washed and torn

3 avocadoes, halved and cut into large dice

To make the vinaigrette: Place the oils, vinegar, salt and pepper in a small mixing bowl and mix well.

Prepare the grill or preheat the broiler.

Place the pineapple slices 4 inches from the heat source and cook until golden, about 3 to 5 minutes on each side. Cut each slice into 8 triangles.

Divide the watercress between 6 salad plates and top with equal amounts of avocado and pineapple. Drizzle lightly with the vinaigrette. Serve at room temperature.

Jake and Earl's Six-Layer Bars with Chocolate, Pecans and Coconut

Chris Schlesinger, chief owner of East Coast Grill, and Cary Wheaton, co-owner of Full Moon, two of my favorite Boston restaurants, used to own Boston's best barbecue joint, Jake and Earl's Dixie BBQ. Jake and Earl's, which is now closed, served these amazing Six Layer Bars, but, for some reason, neither East Coast Grill nor Full Moon continue to carry them. So, if you're dying for one, you've got to make it yourself. Here it is, layer for layer.

If you want to really undo your guests, add some extra layers: 1 cup each of any or all of the following: white chocolate, butterscotch, Heath Bar or toffee chips. Be sure to serve strong coffee.

> ¼ cup unsalted butter, melted
> 12 whole graham crackers (do not use low-fat), crumbled into a powder
> ¾ cup shredded coconut (sweetened or unsweetened is fine)
> 1 cup semisweet chocolate chips
> ¾ cup sweetened condensed milk
> 1 cup toasted pecans, chopped (see page 102)

Preheat the oven to 350 degrees.

Place the butter and graham cracker crumbs in an 8-inch-square pan and combine until they are well incorporated. Press down in an even layer.

Sprinkle ½ cup coconut on the graham cracker crust.

Sprinkle the chocolate chips over the coconut.

Drizzle the condensed milk over the chocolate chips.

Sprinkle the pecans over the condensed milk.

continued on next page

MENU
SIXTEEN

Jake and Earl's Six–Layer Bars with Chocolate, Pecans and Coconut (*cont.*)

Sprinkle the remaining ¼ cup coconut over the pecans and lightly press down. Transfer to the oven and bake for 30 minutes. Set aside to cool. Cut into 9 squares.

Transfer to a platter and serve immediately or cover and store at room temperature overnight.

MENU SEVENTEEN

THREE-BEAN CHILI WITH TONS OF GARNISHES

CORN BREAD

CHIPS AND SALSA

GREEN SALAD WITH CREAMY ORANGE DRESSING

CHEWY MAPLE COOKIES AND VANILLA ICE CREAM

American as apple pie and football games, this is a perfect meal for a Super Bowl Sunday or for après ice skating or skiing. I like it best to serve all the leftover guests from Thanksgiving or Christmas, particularly if you have your main meal in the early part of the day. You can make everything ahead of time and if you have no guests, you can freeze most of it.

TIME TIPS:

MAKE THE CHILI 2 DAYS AHEAD OF TIME.

MAKE THE CREAMY ORANGE DRESSING THE DAY BEFORE.

MAKE THE SALSA 8 HOURS BEFORE.

MAKE THE COOKIES THE DAY BEFORE.

THREE-BEAN CHILI WITH
TONS OF GARNISHES

*I*t is a great relief to make the chili ahead of time since the garnishes can take some time to prepare. If you don't have enough small bowls for the condiments, use hollowed-out orange halves, wine glasses or any small container.

Feel free to throw in leftover turkey, chicken, beef or ham.

1 teaspoon olive or canola oil

2 Spanish onions, coarsely chopped

4 garlic cloves, finely chopped

2 bell peppers, any combinations of colors, coarsely chopped

1 small eggplant, peeled, if desired, and cubed, or 3 zucchini, cubed

1 tablespoon dried Greek oregano

1 teaspoon–1 tablespoon finely chopped canned chipotle chiles

2 teaspoons crushed red pepper flakes

1–2 tablespoons ground cumin

1 teaspoon cayenne pepper (optional)

one 16-ounce can or 2 cups cooked white beans, drained and rinsed

one 16-ounce can or 2 cups cooked black beans, drained and rinsed

four 1-pound cans dark red kidney beans, drained and rinsed

1 cup dried lentils, washed and picked over for stones

two 20-ounce cans whole tomatoes, coarsely chopped, including juice

Garnishes:

1 large red onion, chopped

2–3 red tomatoes, diced

1 bunch scallions, finely chopped

½ cup chopped fresh cilantro leaves

½ cup chopped fresh basil leaves

½ cup sour cream or plain yogurt

½ cup shredded sharp cheddar cheese

½ cup crumbled goat cheese

2 avocadoes, diced

2 limes, quartered

Place a large stockpot over medium heat and when it is hot, add the oil. Add the onions, garlic, peppers, eggplant or zucchini, oregano, chiles, red pepper flakes, cumin and cayenne, and cook until the vegetables are golden, about 10 minutes.

Lower the heat to low, add the beans, lentils and tomatoes and cook, partially covered, for 1 to 2 hours, stirring occasionally.

Transfer to a heated serving bowl and serve immediately or cover and refrigerate for up to 2 days. Reheat gently.

Place the garnishes in small bowls and allow guests to embellish their chili as they please.

MENU
SEVEN-
TEEN

CORN BREAD

*T*his can be made the day before, but I like it hot out of the oven, slathered with unsalted butter and honey.

> *1 cup yellow stone-ground cornmeal*
> *1½ cups all-purpose flour*
> *2 teaspoons baking powder*
> *1 teaspoon kosher salt*
> *2–3 tablespoons honey*
> *2 large eggs, lightly beaten*
> *1½ cups plain yogurt, buttermilk or sour cream*
> *1 cup canned creamed corn (optional)*
> *¼ cup corn oil*

Preheat the oven to 350 degrees. Lightly butter an 8-inch-square baking pan.

Place the cornmeal, flour, baking powder and salt in a large mixing bowl and mix to combine. In a separate bowl, combine the honey, egg, yogurt, creamed corn, if desired, and oil. Add the egg mixture to the flour mixture and stir until just blended.

Spoon the batter into the prepared pan, transfer to the oven and bake until lightly golden, about 45 to 55 minutes. Do not let it brown.

Cut into 9 squares and transfer to a serving platter. Serve immediately.

Green Salad with Creamy Orange Dressing

For the Dressing:

2 tablespoons olive oil

1 tablespoon sherry vinegar

2 tablespoons frozen orange juice concentrate

2 tablespoons goat cheese

1 bunch romaine lettuce, outer leaves discarded, inner leaves torn

1 bunch watercress, well washed and torn

1 head radicchio, torn

1 fennel bulb, cut into large julienne

1 orange, cut into thin slices

1 teaspoon kosher salt

½ teaspoon black pepper

To make the dressing: Place the oil, vinegar, orange juice concentrate and goat cheese in a blender and blend until creamy.

Place the romaine, watercress, radicchio, fennel and orange in a large salad bowl and drizzle with the dressing. Sprinkle with the salt and pepper and serve immediately.

MENU SEVEN-TEEN

CHEWY MAPLE COOKIES
AND VANILLA ICE CREAM

Make a full batch of Chewy Maple Cookies (see page 226) and serve them with scoops of vanilla ice cream. You could also serve Jake and Earl's Six-Layer Bars (see page 157).

Menu Eighteen

Grilled Marinated Flank Steak with Soy, Sherry and Dijon

Potato Cake with Garlic and Olive Oil

Salad of Arugula, Avocado and Mango

Cheesecake with Raspberry Sauce

A takeoff on the classic American steak–house steak and potatoes dinner, this is a great year–round meal. The steak can be grilled in the summer or panfried in the winter; you can substitute Mashed Sweet Potatoes (see page 182) for the Potato Cake. If the cheesecake seems too much, serve fresh raspberries instead.

TIME TIPS:

THE STEAK MARINADE CAN BE MADE 3 DAYS BEFORE.

THE STEAK CAN BE MARINATED THE NIGHT BEFORE OR EARLY IN THE DAY.

THE CHEESECAKE CAN BE MADE UP TO 3 DAYS AHEAD.

THE SALAD DRESSING CAN BE MADE UP TO 2 DAYS BEFORE.

GRILLED MARINATED FLANK STEAK
WITH SOY, SHERRY AND DIJON

I was a vegetarian for fifteen years until one cool, breezy summer night that followed a very hot, very sticky summer day, I visited a friend who was grilling flank steak on his Cambridge deck. The smell of just about anything being grilled is seductive, but the aroma of the steak knocked me right off my feet. I've been eating meat ever since, and although I don't often cook it, it's one of my favorite things to eat at restaurants. I cook it at home on special occasions, always cooking more than I need, because I love to eat it cold the next day, sprinkled with lots of kosher salt and black pepper.

NOTE: when you purchase a steak for marinating, purchase two and freeze one, with the marinade, in a resealable plastic bag. When you are ready to cook it, simply place the bag in the refrigerator to defrost. You'll have a meal with essentially no work.

3 pounds flank steak, skirt steak or London broil

For the Marinade:
2 tablespoons soy sauce
3 tablespoons sherry
3 tablespoons Dijon mustard
¼ cup light brown sugar
1 tablespoon curry powder

1½ teaspoons kosher salt
½–1 teaspoon black pepper
3 scallions, chopped, for garnish

Score both sides of the steak with a very sharp knife.

Place the soy sauce, sherry, mustard, sugar and curry powder in a large shallow glass or ceramic bowl and add the steak, turning it once so that both sides are covered. Cover and let sit at room temperature no more than 2 hours or refrigerate 4 hours or up to overnight, turning occasionally.

Prepare the grill or broiler.

Remove and reserve as much marinade as possible and place it in a small saucepan. Bring to a boil and set aside.

Sprinkle the steak with the salt and pepper and place it on the grill or under the broiler, and cook until deeply browned and crusty, about 5 minutes per side, basting occasionally with the reserved marinade.

Cut into 6 big squares and divide evenly between 6 plates. Serve immediately. Garnish with the scallions.

MENU
EIGHTEEN

Potato Cake with Garlic and Olive Oil

*M*ashed potatoes with flair.

Note: you can substitute Mashed Sweet Potatoes (see page 182).

2½ pounds red new potatoes, peeled, if desired, and quartered
1 tablespoon olive oil
6–8 garlic cloves, finely chopped
1–1½ teaspoons kosher salt
¼–½ teaspoon black pepper
¼ cup unsalted butter, at room temperature

Preheat the oven to 450 degrees. Lightly oil an 8-inch-square baking dish.

Place the potatoes in a large stockpot and cover with cold water. Bring to a boil over high heat, lower the heat to medium and cook, uncovered, until the potatoes are tender, about 20 to 25 minutes.

While the potatoes are cooking, place the oil in a large skillet over very low heat and when it is hot, add the garlic. Cook until golden, about 5 to 10 minutes, being careful not to let it brown. Set aside.

Drain the potatoes and mash them with a fork until they are some-what chunky. Add the garlic and oil mixture, salt, pepper and butter. Place in the prepared pan, transfer to the oven and bake, uncovered, for 12 minutes. Cut into 6 to 9 squares and serve immediately.

Salad of Arugula, Avocado and Mango

You can substitute almost any salad in this meal, but this bitter, buttery and sweet salad works particularly well.

For the Dressing:
2 tablespoons olive oil
1 tablespoon red wine vinegar
1 tablespoon balsamic vinegar
1 teaspoon kosher salt
½ teaspoon black pepper

2 bunches arugula, well washed and torn
2 avocadoes, cut into medium dice
2 mangoes, cut into medium dice

To make the dressing: Place the oil, vinegars, salt and pepper in a small mixing bowl and whisk.

Divide the arugula between 6 plates and top with equal amounts of avocado and mango. Drizzle with the dressing and serve immediately.

MENU
EIGHTEEN

CHEESECAKE WITH RASPBERRY SAUCE

I first made this *Joy of Cooking*–inspired recipe when I was in high school and after trying many other versions, I still feel that there is none better. Later, when I was in college and came home for vacations, I used to make this for my brother Peter, who was then a tall, skinny teenager with a frighteningly voracious appetite. Not one to wait for anything, he rarely allowed it to chill and instead, promptly devoured the whole thing. I wanted him to wait for it to be just right, but even so I was flattered at his inability to do so.

Joy of Cooking authors Rombauer and Becker say this recipe serves twelve, Peter says one, and I say somewhere around eight.

For the Crust:

1¼ cups ground graham crackers or gingersnaps (if you are using small gingersnaps you will need to start with about 2 cups)

¼ cup confectioners' sugar, sifted

5 tablespoons melted unsalted butter

1 teaspoon ground cinnamon

For the Cream Cheese Layer:

2 large eggs

¾ pound cream cheese, at room temperature

½ cup sugar

½ teaspoon vanilla extract

1 teaspoon fresh lemon juice

½ teaspoon kosher salt

For the Sour Cream Layer:

1½ cups sour cream

2 tablespoons sugar

½ teaspoon vanilla extract
⅛ teaspoon kosher salt

2 cups fresh or frozen raspberries
6 strawberries
1 kiwi, cut into 6 slices
12 toasted pecans (see page 102)

Preheat the oven to 375 degrees.

To make the crust: Place the cookie crumbs, confectioners' sugar, butter and cinnamon in a medium–size mixing bowl and stir until they are well incorporated. Press into a 9–inch pie pan. Cover and refrigerate at least 2 hours and up to 24 hours.

To make the cream cheese layer: Place the eggs, cream cheese, sugar, vanilla, lemon juice and salt in a food processor fitted with a steel blade and process well. Pour over the crust.

Transfer to the oven and bake for 20 minutes. Set aside to cool.

To make the sour cream layer: Place the sour cream, sugar, vanilla and salt in a food processor fitted with a steel blade and mix well. Pour over the cooled cream cheese layer, cover and refrigerate at least overnight and up to 3 days.

To make the raspberry sauce: Place the raspberries in a blender or food processor fitted with a steel blade and puree. Set aside.

When cooled, cut the cheesecake into 8 to 12 pieces. Place a slice of cheesecake on each of 6 plates and garnish with a strawberry, a slice of kiwi and 2 pecans. Pour a small puddle of raspberry sauce on the side and serve immediately.

MENU
EIGHTEEN

GRILLED SALMON STEAKS WITH CITRUS AND THYME

PAN-STEAMED SPINACH

LEEK MASHED POTATOES

ENGAGEMENT BROWNIES

The fresh clean flavors of this menu make it a great meal for a cool summer evening.

TIME TIPS:

THE BROWNIES MAY BE PREPARED ONE DAY BEFORE AND STORED TIGHTLY COVERED AT ROOM TEMPERATURE.

GRILLED SALMON STEAKS WITH CITRUS AND THYME

I got this recipe from my friend Nancy Olin, who got it from her stepfather, Bob Raives, who cut it out of a newspaper, but he no longer remembers which one. It's gone through enough changes to avoid a lawsuit, but if you're the author, my congratulations on an amazing dish and my apologies for not acknowledging you.

> *1 tablespoon grated lemon zest*
>
> *1 tablespoon grated lime zest*
>
> *2 garlic cloves, minced*
>
> *1½ tablespoons chopped fresh Italian flat-leaf parsley leaves*
>
> *1½ tablespoon fresh thyme leaves*
>
> *1½ teaspoons kosher salt*
>
> *1 teaspoon black pepper*
>
> *six 6–8 ounce (about 2½–3 pounds) salmon steaks*
>
> *6 Italian flat-leaf parsley sprigs, for garnish*
>
> *1 lemon, thinly sliced, for garnish*
>
> *1 lime, thinly sliced, for garnish*

Place the lemon zest, lime zest, garlic, parsley, thyme, salt and pepper on a large plate and mash them together to form a paste. Add the salmon, coat with the paste, cover and let sit for 1 hour.

Prepare the grill.

Place the steaks on a rack on the grill and cook until browned, about 4 to 5 minutes on each side. Transfer to 6 plates, each with a bed of Pan-Steamed Spinach (see page 175), and serve immediately. Garnish with the parsley, lemon and lime.

Pan-Steamed Spinach

If you serve the salmon on top of the spinach, which is the way I recommend, you can give it a fancy name like Salmon à la Florentine. When dishes are served on a bed of spinach, they are called Florentine because when Catherine de Médicis left her home in Florence in the 1500s to marry the king of France she brought along her own cooks to prepare spinach, her favorite vegetable. Lacking a wealth of recipe ideas and needing some versatility, they often served the spinach underneath whatever they were making. Nevertheless, this is a great way to serve spinach.

> *2–3 pounds bunch spinach, trimmed*
> *1 tablespoon olive oil*
> *4 garlic cloves, chopped*
> *1 teaspoon kosher salt*
> *¼–½ teaspoon black pepper*

Wash the spinach well and shake out the excess water. Place a large saucepan over high heat and add the wet spinach. Cook, stirring occasionally, until the spinach is tender, about 5 to 7 minutes. Transfer the spinach to a colander and set aside.

Reheat the saucepan over medium heat and add the oil. Add the garlic and cook until golden, about 3 minutes. Add the cooked spinach, toss to combine and cook until heated through, about 2 minutes. Add the salt and pepper. Serve immediately.

MENU
NINETEEN

Leek Mashed Potatoes

Leeks, which are sweeter and more subtle than onions, are said to last in the refrigerator for two weeks, but I find that they often become slimy, so I purchase them only when I need them.

Most books recommend that you wash leeks under cold running water, but I've discovered that rinsing in hot water works better for getting the dirt out. Since most of the time you are going to cook them, it doesn't affect their taste or texture. Trim off the roots and all but the first inch or so of green, slice the leek lengthwise, open it up and rinse several times.

2 tablespoons unsalted butter
1 bunch leeks, white part only, finely chopped
2 pounds new potatoes, peeled, if desired, and diced
2½–3 cups cold water
2–4 tablespoons heavy cream
¾ teaspoon kosher salt
¼–½ teaspoon white pepper

Place a large skillet over medium heat and when it is hot, add the butter. Add the leeks and cook until they are soft and golden, about 12 minutes. Raise the heat to high, add the potatoes and 2½ cups of the water and bring to a boil. Cook until the potatoes are tender, about 20 to 25 minutes. If necessary, add the remaining ½ cup water. Mash with a fork or potato masher and gradually add the cream, salt and pepper. Reheat over very low heat, if necessary. Serve immediately.

Engagement Brownies

*E*ven before my husband proposed to me, his father did. He tasted these brownies and wanted to be sure he had a steady supply.

Serve with coffee ice cream, if you can stand it.

For the Brownies:
5 tablespoons unsalted butter

6 ounces bittersweet or semisweet chocolate

2 large eggs

¾ cup sugar

2 teaspoons vanilla extract

⅔ cup all-purpose flour

2 tablespoons unsweetened cocoa powder, such as Droste or Callebaut

½ teaspoon baking powder

¼ teaspoon kosher salt

For the Glaze:
1½ teaspoons unsalted butter

1 teaspoon light corn syrup

⅓ cup confectioners' sugar

3 tablespoons water

3 ounces bittersweet or semisweet chocolate

1 ounce unsweetened chocolate

1 teaspoon vanilla extract

Preheat the oven to 350 degrees. Lightly butter an 8 x 8-inch pan.

To make the brownies: Place the butter and chocolate in a medium–

continued on next page

MENU
NINETEEN

Engagement Brownies (*cont.*)

size saucepan and cook over the lowest possible heat until melted. Set aside to cool.

While the chocolate is cooling, place the eggs, sugar and vanilla in a medium-size bowl and whisk until frothy.

When the chocolate has cooled to room temperature, add the egg mixture. Add the flour, cocoa powder, baking powder and salt and mix to combine.

Transfer to the prepared pan, place in the oven and bake until firm, about 25 to 30 minutes. Set aside to cool.

To prepare the glaze: Place the butter, corn syrup, sugar and water in a medium-size pan and bring to a boil over high heat. Add the chocolates and vanilla and stir until smooth. Set aside to cool.

When the brownie has cooled, spread the glaze over the brownie and let it set until the glaze is cooled. Cut into 9 to 12 squares.

SPICY MUSTARD STEAK TIPS

MASHED SWEET POTATOES

SEARED GREENS

CHOCOLATE MOUSSE TORTE

One night last winter I was dying for steak but couldn't quite figure out how I wanted it cooked. So I just bought the steak tips and figured I'd wing it when I got home. The main ingredients that go into this are some of my favorite flavors and the ones you can always find in my kitchen: chipotle chile powder, mustard and lime juice. Of course you can use actual chipotle chiles, if you want the extra work of soaking, seeding and pureeing the peppers, but I use the powder because it's easy. The mashed sweet potatoes and seared greens make this a classic American dinner with pumped-up flavors.

TIME TIPS:

MAKE THE STEAK MARINADE UP TO 2 DAYS BEFORE.

MAKE THE MASHED SWEET POTATOES THE DAY BEFORE AND GENTLY REHEAT.

MAKE THE CHOCOLATE MOUSSE TORTE THE DAY BEFORE.

SPICY MUSTARD STEAK TIPS

*B*e careful not to overmarinate the tips or they'll get stringy. Alternatively, you can cook the tips without the mustard mixture and then toss them with it afterwards.

At an average cost of $5.99 per pound (at this writing), steak tips are no cheaper than steak, but I like the way these look with the mashed sweet potatoes. You can substitute the same amount of whole sirloin steaks, and cook them about five minutes per side instead of two to three.

If you like chipotle chiles, you'll love chipotle chile powder, available by mail order from Penzey's Spices in Wisconsin (414-574-0277). No need to soak or puree the chiles, just shake the jar.

> ⅓ cup Dijon mustard
> ¾ teaspoon chipotle chile powder
> juice of ½ lime
> 1½ teaspoons light brown sugar
> 3 pounds thinly sliced sirloin steak tips
> 1½ teaspoons kosher salt
> ½ teaspoon black pepper
> 1 tablespoon olive oil
> ½ bunch scallions, chopped, for garnish

Place the mustard, chipotle chile powder, lime juice and brown sugar in a large glass or ceramic mixing bowl and stir well. Add the sirloin tips and set aside.

Remove the excess marinade from the steak and sprinkle with the salt and pepper.

Place a large skillet over medium–high heat and when it is hot, add the oil. Add the tips, once piece at a time, allowing the pan to reheat for about 10 seconds between additions. Cook until well browned, about 2 to 3 minutes on each side. Divide among 6 dinner plates and garnish with the scallions. Serve immediately.

MENU
TWENTY

MASHED SWEET POTATOES

My daughter, Lauren, who has no interest in potatoes, thinks that eating sweet potatoes, either baked or mashed this way, is about the best dinner she could have. Luckily, I, too, could eat these every night.

> *4–5 sweet potatoes, peeled and cut into large dice*
> *2 tablespoons unsalted butter*
> *1–2 tablespoons maple syrup*
> *1 teaspoon kosher salt*

Place the potatoes in a large saucepan, cover with water and bring to a boil over high heat. Boil until the sweet potatoes are tender, about 20 minutes.

Drain well, transfer to a bowl or a food processor fitted with a steel blade and mix until pureed. Add the butter, maple syrup and salt and mix well.

SEARED GREENS

1 tablespoon olive oil

2–3 garlic cloves, minced

*1 bunch mustard greens, broccoli rabe, spinach or escarole, well washed
and trimmed*

2 tablespoons balsamic vinegar

1 teaspoon sugar

1 teaspoon kosher salt

½ teaspoon black pepper

Place the oil in a large skillet over high heat and when it is almost
smoking, add the garlic, greens, vinegar and sugar, stirring well after each
addition. Cook until wilted, about 1 to 2 minutes. Add the salt and pepper.
Transfer to a large heated platter and serve immediately.

MENU
TWENTY

CHOCOLATE MOUSSE TORTE

I've adapted this torte from a recipe by Maida Heatter but I wish I'd invented it myself: it's such a perfect luscious ending to dinner. Half the mousse is cooked to make a crust and the other half is chilled to form the filling.

8 ounces semisweet chocolate, chopped
¼ cup boiling water
8 large eggs, separated (see note)
⅔ cup sugar
1 teaspoon vanilla extract
⅛ teaspoon kosher salt
½ cup whipped cream, for garnish (optional)

Preheat the oven to 350 degrees. Lightly butter a 9-inch pie pan.

Place the chocolate and boiling water in a small mixing bowl and stir until the chocolate melts. Set aside to cool.

Place the egg yolks in the bowl of a mixer and beat until lemon colored, about 3 to 5 minutes. Gradually, while the mixer is running, add the sugar, vanilla and the cooled chocolate mixture.

Place the egg whites in the bowl of a mixer and beat until they form stiff peaks. Gradually fold into the chocolate mixture. Transfer 4 cups to a medium-size mixing bowl, cover and refrigerate. Place the remaining mousse in the prepared pan and bake for 25 minutes. Cool to room temperature and then cover and refrigerate until completely chilled, about 30 minutes. Place the reserved mousse on the mousse in the pie pan and cover and refrigerate for at least 3 hours and up to overnight. Garnish with whipped cream, if desired.

NOTE: The use of raw eggs carries the risk of salmonella. No recipe using raw eggs should be served to the very young, the very old, or anyone with a compromised immune system.

MENU TWENTY-ONE

BOUILLABAISSE WITH ROUILLE

FRENCH BREAD

ROMAINE SALAD WITH ARUGULA, ROQUEFORT CHEESE AND PEARS

VANILLA ICE CREAM WITH BITTERSWEET CHOCOLATE SAUCE AND RASPBERRIES

I went to France when I was a teenager, more concerned with finding great beaches than finding great food. Regretfully I never had bouillabaisse when I was there. Bouillabaisse, a celebrated seafood stew from Provence, is one of those dishes about which people have long heated debates. Do you use "throwaway" fish or only the best? Do you add potatoes? I am not attempting authenticity here, only to make something that tastes yummy. In France they use local fish, so be sure to do the same.

TIME TIPS:

THE BOUILLABAISSE BASE AND ROUILLE CAN BE MADE A DAY AHEAD.

THE BITTERSWEET CHOCOLATE SAUCE CAN BE MADE 2 DAYS AHEAD.

BOUILLABAISSE WITH ROUILLE

Most recipes for bouillabaisse call for fish broth to be made as the first part of the recipe. If you are the type to make fish broth, you probably have a recipe for it; if not, no recipe I could include would induce you to make it. You can go to a good fish market or specialty store and purchase ready-made fish broth or substitute a mixture of two cups bottled clam juice and two cups water.

Rouille is a spicy red pepper and garlic mayonnaise–type sauce from Provence.

For the Bouillabaisse:

2 tablespoons olive oil

2 Spanish onions, chopped

4 garlic cloves, minced

1–2 fennel bulbs, diced

3 carrots, chopped

2 celery stalks, chopped

one 28-ounce can tomatoes, chopped, including the juice

zest of ½ orange, cut into julienne

2 bay leaves

1 teaspoon dried thyme

2–3 teaspoons fennel seed

2 cups diced potatoes

4 cups chicken broth

4 cups fish broth

pinch saffron, or more to taste

4 tablespoons Pernod, anisette or sambuca

For the Rouille:

1 roasted red pepper, cut into large dice (see page 37)

2 garlic cloves

1 slice white bread

1 tablespoon warm water

¼ cup olive oil

¼ cup vegetable oil

½ teaspoon kosher salt

¼ teaspoon cayenne pepper

1 pound lean fish, such as cod, monkfish or halibut, cut into big
    chunks

2 pounds mussels, cleaned and debearded

½ pound scallops, quartered

1 pound large shrimp, peeled and deveined

¼ cup chopped fresh Italian flat-leaf parsley leaves, for garnish

¼ cup chopped fresh basil leaves, for garnish

1 tablespoon fresh thyme leaves, for garnish

To make the Bouillabaisse: Place a large skillet over medium heat and when it is hot, add the oil. Add the onions, garlic, fennel, carrots and celery and cook, stirring occasionally, until all are wilted, about 10 minutes. Add the tomatoes, orange zest, bay leaves, thyme, fennel and potatoes and cook for 5 minutes. Raise the heat to medium–high and add the broths, saffron and 2 tablespoons Pernod, and cook for 5 minutes. Lower the heat to low and cook until the stew has come together and reduced somewhat, about 1 hour.

While the bouillabaisse is cooking, make the rouille: Place the red pepper, garlic and bread in a food processor fitted with a steel blade and

continued on next page

MENU
TWENTY-
ONE

Bouillabaisse with Rouille (*cont.*)

process until well chopped. Add the water and pulse to combine. Gradually, while the machine is running, add the oils, salt and cayenne pepper
and mix until thick. Set aside.

If you are cooking this a day ahead, cover and refrigerate. If not, add
the fish, mussels, scallops and shrimp, cover and cook until the fish is
cooked, about 10 minutes.

Just prior to serving, add the remaining 2 tablespoons Pernod. Transfer
to 6 heated shallow bowls and serve immediately. Garnish with the parsley, basil and thyme and drizzle with rouille.

Romaine Salad with Arugula, Roquefort Cheese and Pears

This salad is a perfect combination of texture and flavor. I could eat it every night and with almost anything. Feel free to replace the pear with an apple or my current favorite, pink grapefruit sections.

> *2 tablespoons balsamic vinegar*
> *2 tablespoons olive oil*
> *½ teaspoon Dijon mustard*
> *2 heads romaine lettuce, outer leaves discarded, inside leaves torn*
> *2 bunches arugula, well washed and torn*
> *¼–½ cup crumbled Roquefort cheese*
> *1 large pear, peeled, if desired, and thinly sliced*
> *1 teaspoon kosher salt*
> *½ teaspoon black pepper*

Place the vinegar, oil and mustard in a small mixing bowl and mix to combine.

Place the romaine and arugula in a large salad bowl and toss. Add the Roquefort cheese and pear and toss well. Drizzle with the dressing and sprinkle with the salt and pepper. Serve immediately.

MENU
TWENTY-
ONE

Vanilla Ice cream with Bittersweet Chocolate Sauce and Raspberries

When I say bittersweet I really mean it: this sauce is a perfect bitter contrast to the sweet creamy ice cream. If you want it a little sweeter, add an extra tablespoon or two of sugar. This is also great drizzled on pound cake.

> *½ cup unsweetened cocoa powder, such as Droste or Callebaut*
> *2 cups heavy cream*
> *2 tablespoons sugar*
> *6 cups vanilla ice cream*
> *½ pint fresh raspberries*

Place the cocoa, cream and sugar in a small saucepan and bring to a low boil over medium–high heat. Cook, stirring constantly, until it just begins to thicken, about 3 to 5 minutes.

Place the ice cream in individual bowls or wine glasses, drizzle with the hot sauce and serve immediately. Garnish with the raspberries.

TUNA AU POIVRE
ROASTED RATATOUILLE
ROASTED NEW POTATOES
FRENCH BREAD
NECTARINE, STRAWBERRY AND BLUEBERRY CRUNCH

*A*lthough most of this menu was inspired by the flavors of Provence (*poivre* is the French word for pepper), the dessert is 100 percent American, making this a wonderful summer dinner. You can serve polenta or steamed rice instead of potatoes, if you prefer.

TIME TIPS:

MARINATE THE TUNA UP TO 2 HOURS AHEAD.

CUT UP THE POTATOES AND PLACE THEM IN A BOWL WITH THE OIL IN THE AFTERNOON.

CUT UP THE RATATOUILLE VEGETABLES AND PLACE THEM IN A BOWL WITH THE OIL IN THE AFTERNOON.

ASSEMBLE THE NECTARINE, STRAWBERRY AND BLUEBERRY CRUNCH UP TO 4 HOURS IN ADVANCE AND BAKE IT WHILE YOU EAT DINNER.

Tuna au Poivre

Cynthia Stuart, one of my oldest and dearest friends, gave me this recipe. It's pure Cynthia: low in calories and fat, deceptively easy to make, pretty to look at, high in flavor and jammed with black pepper. It's also great made with salmon.

2½–3 pounds tuna steak, about 1–1¼ inches thick
¼ cup soy sauce
2 garlic cloves, finely chopped
juice of 1½ limes
½ teaspoon sugar
1 tablespoon olive oil
4 teaspoons coarsely ground black pepper
1 lime, thinly sliced, for garnish

Place the tuna steaks in a shallow glass or ceramic bowl and cover with the soy sauce, garlic, lime juice and sugar. Cover and refrigerate for no more than 2 hours or at room temperature for 1 hour, turning occasionally. Discard the excess marinade.

Coat both sides of the tuna with the pepper, pressing in a bit. Place a large nonstick skillet over high heat and when it is hot, add the oil. Add the tuna steaks, one at a time, allowing the pan to reheat for about 30 seconds between additions. Cook for about 3 minutes on each side for rare tuna or 5 minutes for well done. Transfer to individual plates and serve immediately. Garnish with the lime.

Roasted Ratatouille

Ratatouille is a great dish for experimentation. Although the usual method is to sauté the vegetables, I find that roasting them nets an even richer result.

1 large Spanish onion, chopped
1–2 garlic cloves, chopped
3 zucchini, diced
1 large Sicilian or 4 Japanese eggplants, peeled, if desired, and diced
1 tablespoon olive oil
1 teaspoon kosher salt
½ teaspoon black pepper
2 cups diced fresh Roma, canned whole or fresh cherry tomatoes
1 teaspoon dried Greek oregano
¼–½ teaspoon crushed red pepper flakes (optional)
2 tablespoons chopped fresh basil leaves
2 tablespoons chopped fresh Italian flat-leaf parsley leaves
1 tablespoon balsamic vinegar

Preheat the oven to 400 degrees.

Place the onion, garlic, zucchini and eggplant on a large baking sheet and toss with the oil, salt and pepper. Cook until they are tender and just beginning to brown, about 35 minutes. Add the tomatoes, oregano and the red pepper flakes, if desired, and cook 10 minutes.

Just prior to serving, add the basil, parsley and vinegar. Serve hot, at room temperature or chilled.

Menu Twenty-Two

ROASTED NEW POTATOES

*G*arlic and rosemary make this simple side dish something special.

2½–3 pounds new potatoes, quartered or halved

2 tablespoons olive oil

4 garlic cloves, minced

1 teaspoon kosher salt

½ teaspoon black pepper

1 tablespoon chopped fresh rosemary leaves

Preheat the oven to 400 degrees.

Place the potatoes, oil, garlic, salt and pepper on a large roasting pan or baking sheet and toss to combine.

Transfer to the oven and roast until golden, about 40 minutes.

Transfer to a large heated serving bowl and serve immediately. Garnish with the rosemary.

Nectarine, Strawberry and Blueberry Crunch

This is the kind of dessert I can't refuse. Feel free to substitute different fruits or add a drizzle of heavy cream or a dollop of ice cream.

6 nectarines, peeled, pitted and thinly sliced
1 pint fresh strawberries, hulled and quartered
1 pint fresh blueberries
1 tablespoon chopped fresh mint leaves
⅔ cup all-purpose flour
⅔ cup old-fashioned rolled oats
3 tablespoons light brown sugar
3 tablespoons sugar
¼ teaspoon kosher salt
¼ cup unsalted butter, melted

Preheat the oven to 350 degrees.

Place the nectarines, strawberries, blueberries and mint in an ungreased 8 x 8–inch baking pan and toss to combine.

Place the flour, oats, sugars, salt and butter in a small mixing bowl and combine, by hand or with two forks, until the mixture is crumbly. Place the mixture on top of the fruit and transfer the pan to the oven. Bake until the top is golden brown, about 35 minutes. Serve warm, at room temperature or chilled.

Menu Twenty-Two

MENU TWENTY-THREE

CHICKEN FRICASSEE
EGG NOODLES OR RICE
STEAMED FRESH PEAS
APPLE CRISP

I always think of fricassee as French, but it really originated in the American South. If you can't find good fresh peas, use frozen baby peas, not canned.

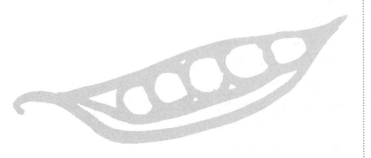

TIME TIPS:

MAKE THE CHICKEN FRICASSEE THE DAY BEFORE.

MAKE THE APPLE CRISP IN THE AFTERNOON.

Chicken Fricassee

*O*ld-fashioned but wonderful. This is a perfect example of why classic dishes never die.

You can add the steamed peas directly to the fricassee, or serve them on the side. I'm assuming you'll know how to do this—I've not included a recipe.

> *1 fryer chicken, about 4–4½ pounds, cut into 8 pieces, trimmed of excess fat*
>
> *1½–2 pounds any combination of chicken breasts, legs and thighs, trimmed of excess fat*
>
> *1 large Spanish onion, sliced*
>
> *4 garlic cloves, thinly sliced*
>
> *4 celery stalks, cut into thick julienne*
>
> *1 pound carrots, peeled, if desired, and cut into thick julienne*
>
> *1 pound button mushrooms, sliced or chopped*
>
> *1½ teaspoons dried thyme*
>
> *2 bay leaves*
>
> *5 tablespoons all-purpose flour*
>
> *1 cup dry white vermouth*
>
> *5 cups chicken broth*
>
> *2 tablespoons heavy cream (optional)*
>
> *2 tablespoons fresh lemon juice*
>
> *2 teaspoons fresh thyme leaves*
>
> *¼ cup chopped fresh Italian flat-leaf parsley leaves*

Place a large nonstick skillet or cast-iron Dutch oven over medium-high heat and, when it is hot, add the chicken pieces, one at a time, allowing the pan to reheat for about 30 seconds between additions, and cook until well browned, about 3 to 4 minutes on each side. This will take at least two to three batches. Transfer the chicken to a large plate and set aside. Discard all but 1 teaspoon of fat.

Reheat the pan, add the onion and garlic and cook until they are soft and golden, about 3 to 5 minutes. Add the celery, carrots, mushrooms, thyme and bay leaves and cook until the carrots begin to soften, about 10 minutes. Sprinkle the flour over the vegetables, one tablespoon at a time, stirring all the while.

When the flour has been completely incorporated, gradually add the vermouth and the broth. Return the chicken to the skillet. Lower the heat to very, very low and cook for 1 to 1½ hours, stirring occasionally. Discard the bay leaves.

Cover and refrigerate overnight.

Just prior to serving, add the cream, if desired, and the lemon juice, thyme and parsley.

MENU
TWENTY-
THREE

APPLE CRISP

This is a very simple, homey dessert that is easy to make and satisfying to eat. And you can substitute almost any fruit: pears, plums, peaches or nectarines and combine them with strawberries, raspberries or blueberries.

For the Apples:

6 Granny Smith apples, peeled, cored, quartered and thinly sliced

1 tablespoon all-purpose flour

1 tablespoon sugar

For the Topping:

¾ cup all-purpose flour

½ cup old-fashioned rolled oats

3 tablespoons light brown sugar

3 tablespoons sugar

1 teaspoon ground cinnamon

¼ teaspoon kosher salt

Preheat the oven to 350 degrees.

To prepare the apples: Place the apples, 1 tablespoon flour and 1 tablespoon sugar in an ungreased 9 x 12-inch baking dish and toss to combine.

To make the topping: Place the ¾ cup flour, oats, brown sugar, 3 tablespoons sugar, cinnamon and salt in a medium-size mixing bowl and toss to combine. Pour the mixture over the apples, distribute evenly and pat down gently. Transfer the pan to the oven and bake until the apples are soft and the topping is lightly browned, about 1 hour. Serve hot or at room temperature.

MENU TWENTY-FOUR

CHILLED SUMMER MINESTRONE

ITALIAN BREAD

GRILLED SHRIMP SKEWERS

LEMON-GLAZED PECAN AND COCONUT SQUARES

When it's too hot to eat but you need to serve something, this is a great menu, full of intense but light flavors.

TIME TIPS:

THE MINESTRONE CAN BE MADE 2 DAYS AHEAD.

THE LEMON-GLAZED PECAN AND COCONUT SQUARES CAN BE MADE THE DAY BEFORE.

CHILLED SUMMER MINESTRONE

*T*his soup uses the best vegetables of spring and summer. For me, it's enough to serve it alone with bread. But the addition of the shrimp skewers makes it more substantial and special.

> *1 teaspoon olive oil*
> *½ Spanish onion, chopped*
> *2 celery stalks, including leaves, chopped*
> *1 garlic clove, minced*
> *1 cup fresh shelled fava beans, or shelled lima beans (start with about*
> *   1 pound)*
> *3½ cups chicken broth*
> *1 cup fresh peas (start with about 1 pound)*
> *1 bunch asparagus, trimmed and chopped*
> *1 cup fresh corn kernels (start with 1–2 cobs)*
> *⅔ cup freshly grated Parmesan cheese*
> *⅓ cup heavy cream*
> *1 large beefsteak tomato, chopped*
> *⅓–½ cup chopped fresh basil leaves*
> *kosher salt*
> *black pepper*

Place a large stockpot over medium-high heat and when it is hot, add the oil. Add the onion, celery and garlic and cook for 5 minutes. Add the beans and broth and bring to a boil. Lower the heat to low and cook until the beans are soft, about 15 to 20 minutes.

Off heat, add the peas, asparagus, corn and Parmesan cheese and stir until the Parmesan has melted. Set aside to cool to room temperature.

Transfer 1 to 1½ cups of the solids to a blender and add the cream.

Process until smooth and return to the stockpot. (If you want a smooth soup, blend all of it at this point.) Add the tomato, basil, salt and pepper to taste.

Transfer to a large serving bowl, cover and refrigerate at least 2 hours and up to 2 days.

MENU
TWENTY-
FOUR

GRILLED SHRIMP SKEWERS

24 large shrimp, peeled and deveined
2 tablespoons olive oil
1 teaspoon kosher salt
½ teaspoon black pepper

Prepare the grill. Place 6 wooden skewers in a bowl of water and let them soak.

Place the shrimp, oil, salt and pepper in a medium-size mixing bowl and toss to coat.

Thread 4 shrimp onto each skewer. Place the skewers on the grill and cook until the shrimp are pink and opaque throughout, about 2 to 3 minutes per side. Lay the skewers across the soup and serve immediately.

Lemon-Glazed Pecan and Coconut Squares

*V*ery tart and very sweet.

For the Crust:

1 ½ cups all-purpose flour

3 tablespoons sugar

½ teaspoon kosher salt

½ cup unsalted butter

For the Pecan and Coconut Filling:

3 large eggs

1 ½ cups dark brown sugar

¾ cup chopped pecans

¾ cup shredded unsweetened coconut

1 ½ teaspoons vanilla extract

For the Lemon Glaze:

½ cup confectioners' sugar

¼ cup fresh lemon juice

2 teaspoons grated lemon zest

Preheat the oven to 350. Lightly butter a 12 x 8-inch pan.

To make the crust: Place the flour, sugar, salt and butter in a bowl or a food processor fitted with a steel blade and mix until well combined. Place in the prepared pan, transfer to the oven and bake until just golden, about 15 minutes. Set aside to cool.

To make the filling: Place the eggs, brown sugar, pecans, coconut and vanilla in a small mixing bowl and combine well. Pour over the cooled

continued on next page

Menu
Twenty-
Four

Lemon–Glazed Coconut Squares (*cont.*)

crust, transfer to the oven and bake until slightly browned, about 20 to 30 minutes.

   To make the glaze: Place the confectioners' sugar, lemon juice and lemon zest in a small mixing bowl and combine. Pour over the filling while it is warm and still in the pan.

   Cut into 12 pieces and serve warm or at room temperature. Place onto a large platter.

SPICY SCALLOPS WITH CASHEWS

STEAMED BASMATI RICE

WATERCRESS SALAD WITH ORANGE SEGMENTS

VANILLA ICE CREAM WITH ROASTED PEACHES
AND GINGERROOT

When I worked at The Legal Sea Foods Marketplace, I worked with a woman named Quan who use to sneak into the restaurant kitchen and make us unbelievable lunches. Having never seen ketchup used in Asian cooking, I was surprised and intrigued and actually couldn't quite imagine how great a dish this would be. It turned out to be one of my favorite lunches and I begged her to make it at least once a week. She was the first person to introduce me to Vietnamese chili paste and now I am never without it.

If you want a hot vegetable instead of a salad you can substitute sautéed snow peas or bunch spinach. Or if you're feeling extravagant, you could serve both.

TIME TIPS:

MAKE THE SAUCE FOR THE SPICY SCALLOPS WITH CASHEWS THE DAY BEFORE.

Spicy Scallops with Cashews

Don't be intimidated by the long list of ingredients—most of them can be found in your pantry. The Asian ingredients can be found in a well-stocked supermarket or specialty foods store. If you have to buy them just for this dish it may push you over the $50 mark, but they keep indefinitely and you'll find lots of ways to use them in everyday cooking. The versatile sauce can be used with shrimp and as a finishing or basting sauce for grilled scallops, shrimp or chicken. It can be prepared right before you cook or hours ahead, which makes it a sure bet when you don't have a lot of time.

For the Sauce:
3 tablespoons dry sherry
⅓ cup ketchup
3 tablespoons oyster sauce
¾ teaspoon toasted sesame oil
2 teaspoons rice or red wine vinegar
¾–1 teaspoon Vietnamese chili paste

1½ teaspoons cornstarch
1½ teaspoons cold water

⅔–1 cup toasted cashews, coarsely chopped (see page 102)
½ bunch scallions, cut into julienne
¾ teaspoon grated orange zest

1 tablespoon vegetable oil
2¾–3 pounds sea scallops, patted dry with a towel
3 garlic cloves, minced
2 teaspoons chopped fresh gingerroot

To make the sauce: Place the sherry, ketchup, oyster sauce, sesame oil, vinegar and chili paste in a small mixing bowl and set aside.

Place the cornstarch and water in a small mixing bowl and set aside.

Place the cashews, scallions and orange zest in a small mixing bowl and set aside.

Place a large skillet over medium–high heat and when it is hot, add the vegetable oil. Add the scallops, garlic and gingerroot. Cook, gently turning, until the scallops are browned on all sides, about 4 minutes. Add the sherry mixture and bring to a boil. Add the cornstarch mixture and cook for 1 minute. Transfer to a heated platter and serve immediately. Garnish with the cashews, scallions and orange.

MENU
TWENTY–
FIVE

WATERCRESS SALAD WITH ORANGE SEGMENTS

You could serve this salad separately or with the scallops right on top. You can substitute pink grapefruit, tangerines or clementines.

> 3 bunches watercress, well washed and torn
>
> 2 oranges, diced
>
> 1 tablespoon fresh orange juice
>
> 2 tablespoons rice wine vinegar
>
> 2 tablespoons vegetable oil
>
> 1 teaspoon toasted sesame oil
>
> 1 teaspoon kosher salt
>
> ½ teaspoon black pepper

Place the watercress and oranges in a medium-size salad bowl. Drizzle with the orange juice, vinegar, and oils and sprinkle the salt and pepper. Toss gently and serve immediately.

Vanilla Ice Cream with Roasted Peaches and Gingerroot

¼ cup sugar
1 tablespoon finely chopped fresh gingerroot
½ cup water
6 small peaches, peeled, halved and pitted
2 tablespoons unsalted butter
6 cups vanilla ice cream

Preheat the oven to 400 degrees.

Place the sugar, gingerroot and water in a small saucepan and bring to a boil over high heat. Lower the heat to medium–low and cook for 5 minutes.

Place the peaches in a small baking pan and surround them with the ginger syrup. Dot with the butter.

Transfer to the oven and cook until browned, about 20 minutes.

Divide the ice cream among 6 bowls and top with equal amounts of the hot roasted peaches. Serve immediately.

MENU
TWENTY–
FIVE

MENU TWENTY-SIX

ANA SORTUN'S BRINE-CURED GRILLED PORK LOIN WITH SPANISH TOMATO SALSA

STEAMED RICE

GRILLED ASPARAGUS

CRÈME BRÛLÉE

*J*ust as I was finishing this book, I wrote an article for *The Boston Phoenix* in which I included recipes from three Boston chefs. This Spanish-inspired dinner, from Ana Sortun, the chef at Casablanca, interested me in theory, but I assumed the pork loin would be like most of the pork loins I've had: dull and tasteless. I was so wrong. I loved it so much that I called Ana the next day to ask if I could include it in this book.

TIME TIPS:

MAKE THE BRINE 2 DAYS BEFORE.

MARINATE THE PORK LOIN THE DAY BEFORE.

MAKE THE SALSA IN THE AFTERNOON.

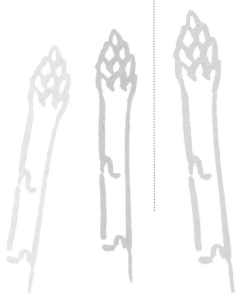

Ana Sortun's Brine-Cured Grilled Pork Loin with Spanish Tomato Salsa

Although the pork must be cured overnight, this is a deceptively easy dish. Simply make the brine, add the pork and forget about it. The next day, about an hour before you're ready to eat, make the salsa and voilà, dinner's on the table.

NOTE: I tested this recipe on the night of a snowstorm and couldn't quite cozy up to the idea of grilling, so I panfried it on a large cast-iron skillet over medium-high heat.

For the Brine:
1 quart cold water
¼ cup white sugar
¼ cup light brown sugar
⅓ cup kosher salt
1½ teaspoons whole black peppercorns
4 juniper berries
2 sprigs fresh rosemary
1 bay leaf
1 small onion, quartered
2 garlic cloves, smashed
pinch fennel seed

4–5-pound pork loin

For the Salsa:
½ red onion, finely minced
¼ cup fresh lemon juice

1 tablespoon sherry vinegar

pinch of sugar

1 small garlic clove, minced

1 green bell pepper, seeded and diced

1 large ripe red tomato, seeds and pulp discarded, remainder diced

1 small ripe yellow tomato, seeds and pulp discarded, remainder diced

½ cup small pitted green olives, whole or halved

¼ cup capers, rinsed

¼ cup chopped fresh cilantro leaves

½ teaspoon chopped fresh oregano leaves

½–1 teaspoon ground cumin

½ teaspoon Hungarian paprika

2 tablespoons extra-virgin olive oil

1 tablespoon olive oil

1 teaspoon kosher salt

½–1 teaspoon black pepper

To make the brine: Place all the ingredients in a large saucepan and bring to a boil over high heat. Transfer to a large glass or ceramic bowl and set aside to cool. When lukewarm, add the pork loin, cover and place in the refrigerator overnight or up to 24 hours.

To make the salsa: Place the onion, lemon juice, vinegar, sugar and garlic in a large glass or ceramic bowl and set aside until the onions turn pink, about 15 minutes. Add the remaining salsa ingredients and set aside for up to 2 hours. Do not refrigerate.

Prepare the grill.

To finish: Remove the pork from the brine, dry it well with a cloth

continued on next page

MENU
TWENTY-
SIX

Ana Sortun's Brine–Cured Grilled Pork Loin with Spanish Tomato Salsa (*cont.*)

towel and trim off excess fat. Cut into 1–inch medallions, brush with the oil and sprinkle with the salt and pepper. Place the medallions on the grill and cook until browned, about 4 minutes on each side. Transfer to heated plates and serve immediately accompanied by the Spanish Tomato Salsa.

GRILLED ASPARAGUS

3 bunches asparagus, trimmed
1–2 tablespoons olive oil
1 teaspoon kosher salt
½ teaspoon black pepper

Prepare the grill.

Place the asparagus, oil, salt and pepper in a medium-size bowl and toss well.

Place the asparagus on the grill and cook until browned, about 5 minutes.

Serve immediately.

MENU
TWENTY–
SIX

CRÈME BRÛLÉE

*I*f you love crème brûlée it's worth investing in individual 4- to 6-ounce ramekins. It doesn't work well in one larger one.

6 large egg yolks
2 large eggs
6 tablespoons light brown sugar
pinch kosher salt
2 teaspoons vanilla extract

½ cup white sugar
1¾ cups heavy cream
1½ cups milk

shaved fresh nutmeg or bittersweet chocolate, for garnish

Preheat the oven to 300 degrees.

Place the egg yolks, eggs, brown sugar, salt and vanilla in a medium-size mixing bowl and mix to combine.

Place the white sugar in a medium-size saucepan over medium heat and cook until it caramelizes. Gradually add the cream and the milk, stirring constantly, until it just begins to boil. Off heat, gradually add the egg mixture and whisk until smooth. Transfer to a strainer and discard the solids. Place in six 4- to 6-ounce ramekins and place the ramekins in a large baking pan. Fill the baking pan with water so that it comes halfway up the sides of the ramekins.

Transfer to the oven and bake until deep golden brown and all but the centers are set, about 1 hour. Serve immediately or cover and refrigerate up to 4 hours. Garnish with the nutmeg or chocolate.

$50 Cookies

I never buy store-made cookies. It's not that I have an attitude about it; it just never occurs to me. And I love to make them, although there was a time when my chocolate chip cookies were so bad (so cakey, so sweet) they were almost inedible.

The following cookie recipes, unless noted, can be formed into logs, covered with plastic wrap or waxed paper and frozen at least one hour and up to one month. They can then be sliced and cooked according to the directions.

CRISPY COCOA COOKIES

*T*hese are my favorite.

MAKES ABOUT 5 DOZEN

> *1 cup unsalted butter, at room temperature*
> *2 cups sugar*
> *2 large eggs*
> *1 tablespoon vanilla extract*
> *1¾ cups all-purpose flour*
> *1 cup high-quality cocoa powder, such as Droste*
> *1 teaspoon baking soda*
> *½ teaspoon baking powder*
> *½ teaspoon kosher salt*
> *1½ cups toasted walnuts, pecans or hazelnuts, chopped (see page 102)*

Preheat the oven to 350 degrees.

Place the butter and sugar in a mixer and process until combined well. Add the eggs and vanilla and mix until just combined. Add the remaining ingredients and process until well incorporated.

Drop by rounded tablespoons onto a large ungreased baking sheet and bake for about 12 to 13 minutes. Do not overbake. Cool the baking sheet between batches.

Cool cookies before storing in an airtight container.

Chocolate Chip Cookies

I have spent literally years and hundreds of dollars coming up with what I think is the perfect chocolate chip cookie. Perfect for me, I should say. I was looking for something that was like the cookie dough I used to slice and bake as a kid and something that was like the kind of cookie that my grandmother's cook, Delia, made. So good, in fact, that it made no difference if you left the chocolate chips out. To me, these are the ideal cookie: crunchy, not too sweet, lots of nuts. If you're looking for soft and chewy, keep looking.

Makes about 5 dozen

> *1 cup unsalted butter, at room temperature*
> *1½ cups sugar*
> *2 large eggs*
> *1 tablespoon vanilla extract*
> *2 cups all-purpose flour*
> *1 teaspoon baking soda*
> *½ teaspoon baking powder*
> *½ teaspoon kosher salt*
> *1 cup semisweet chocolate chips*
> *1½ cups toasted walnuts, pecans or hazelnuts, chopped (see page 102)*

Preheat the oven to 325 degrees.

Place the butter and sugar in a mixer and mix until well combined. Add the eggs and vanilla and mix until just combined. Add the remaining ingredients and mix until well incorporated.

Drop by rounded tablespoons onto a large ungreased baking sheet and bake for about 12 to 13 minutes. Do not overbake. Cool baking sheet between batches.

Cool cookies before storing in an airtight container.

$50 Cookies

GINGERSNAPS

*I*f you like your gingersnaps extra gingery, add one tablespoon finely chopped fresh gingerroot.

MAKES ABOUT 5 DOZEN

> *½ cup unsalted butter, at room temperature*
> *1 cup sugar, plus additional for rolling*
> *1 large egg*
> *3 tablespoons dark molasses*
> *1½ teaspoons vanilla extract*
> *2 cups all-purpose flour*
> *2½–3½ teaspoons ground ginger*
> *1½ teaspoons baking soda*
> *1 teaspoon ground cinnamon*
> *¼ teaspoon kosher salt*

Place the butter and 1 cup sugar in a bowl and mix, by hand or by machine, until light and fluffy.

Add the egg, molasses and vanilla and continue beating until smooth. Gradually beat in the dry ingredients.

To form the cookies, make one large log, roll in white sugar, cover with waxed paper and place in the freezer at least 1 hour and up to 2 weeks.

Preheat the oven to 350 degrees. Lightly butter a cookie sheet.

With the tip of a very sharp knife, slice off thin rounds and place on the prepared baking sheet.

Transfer to the oven and bake until the cookies just begin to brown, about 12 to 14 minutes. If you like your cookies slightly soft, decrease the time and remove from the sheet as soon as they come out of the oven. If you prefer crisp cookies, let the cookies cool on the baking sheet. Cool the baking sheets between batches.

Cool cookies before storing in an airtight container.

Pecan Butter Cookies

Makes about 3 dozen

> 1 cup toasted pecans (about ¾ cup ground) (see page 102)
> 1 cup unsalted butter, at room temperature
> 6 tablespoons sugar
> 2 teaspoons vanilla extract
> 2 cups all-purpose flour
> ½ teaspoon kosher salt
>
> ½ cup confectioners' sugar

Place the pecans, butter, sugar, vanilla, flour and salt in a mixer and mix until well combined. Roll into a ball, cover with plastic wrap and refrigerate until firm.

Preheat the oven to 350 degrees.

Lightly butter a baking sheet. Pull off small walnut–size pieces and form into balls. Flatten the balls and place on the prepared baking sheet. Transfer to the oven and bake until golden brown, about 14 to 16 minutes. Cool the baking sheets between batches. Sprinkle with confectioners' sugar.

Cool cookies before storing in an airtight container.

Hazelnut Shortbread

MAKES ABOUT 4 DOZEN

> 1 cup unsalted butter, at room temperature
>
> ½ cup sugar
>
> ½ cup light brown sugar
>
> 1 teaspoon vanilla extract
>
> 1 cup toasted hazelnuts, finely ground (about ¾ cup ground)
> (see page 102)
>
> 2 cups all-purpose flour
>
> 1 teaspoon kosher salt

Place the butter and sugars in a bowl or a mixer and mix, by hand or by machine, until light and fluffy. Add the vanilla and hazelnuts and continue mixing until smooth. Gradually add the dry ingredients. The batter will seem dry.

To form the cookies, make one large log, and form it into a square column. Cover with waxed paper and place in the freezer at least 1 hour and up to 2 weeks.

Preheat the oven to 350 degrees.

With the tip of a very sharp knife, slice off thin squares and place on an ungreased baking sheet. Transfer to the oven and bake until the cookies are lightly browned, about 12 to 14 minutes. Cool the baking sheet between batches. Do not undercook; these cookies must be completely crisp and toasted.

Cool cookies before storing in an airtight container.

$50
COOKIES

Chewy Maple Cookies

I decided to make molasses cookies one night after putting the kids to bed, but I was out of molasses. So I substituted maple syrup. These cookies turned out to be just what I was looking for: crisp on the edges and chewy in the center.

MAKES ABOUT 5 DOZEN

> *1 cup unsalted butter, at room temperature*
> *1 cup sugar, plus additional for rolling*
> *1 large egg*
> *¾ cup maple syrup*
> *1 teaspoon vanilla extract*
> *2½ cups all-purpose flour*
> *¾ teaspoon kosher salt*
> *¾ teaspoon baking soda*
> *1 teaspoon ground ginger*
> *1½ teaspoons ground cardamom*

Place the butter and sugar in a bowl or a mixer and mix, by hand or by machine, until light and fluffy. Add the egg, maple syrup and vanilla and continue mixing until smooth. Gradually add the dry ingredients.

To form the cookies, make one large log, and roll in sugar. Cover with waxed paper and place in the freezer for at least 1 hour and up to 2 weeks.

Preheat the oven to 350 degrees. Lightly butter a baking sheet.

With the tip of a very sharp knife, slice off thin rounds and place on the prepared baking sheet.

Place in the oven and bake until the cookies just begin to brown, about 12 to 14 minutes. If you like your cookies slightly soft, decrease the time and remove from the sheet as soon as they come out of the oven. If you prefer crisp cookies, let the cookies cool on the baking sheet. Cool the baking sheet between batches.

Cool cookies before storing in an airtight container.

Index

Anchovy Dressing, Romaine Salad with, 135
appetizers and first courses, 31–48
  Asparagus, Fresh, Salad, 120
  Avgolemono Soup, 124
  Bruschetta, 32
  Chickpea Spread, 43
  Corn Soup with Tomatoes, Red Peppers and Cilantro, Chilled, 152
  Minestrone, Chilled Summer, 202–3
  Prosciutto-Wrapped Mango Slices, 146
  Red Onion and Blood Orange Salad, 53
  see also dips
apple(s):
  Crisp, 200
  Granny Smith, Roasted Butternut Squash and, with Walnuts and Currants, 134
Apricots, Dried, Roasted Chicken Breasts with Figs, Prunes and, 114–15
Artichoke and Feta Dip, 34
arugula:
  Romaine Salad with Roquefort Cheese, Pears and, 189
  Salad of Avocado, Mango and, 169
  Salad of Endive, Radicchio and, 83
Asian dishes:
  Baby Back Ribs, Glazed, 140–41
  Cashew Noodles with Asparagus and Peppers, 138–39
  Scallops with Cashews, Spicy, 208–209
  Slaw, 142
  Spicy Sesame Dip, 42

asparagus:
  Cashew Noodles with Peppers and, 138–39
  Fresh, Salad, 120
  Grilled, 217
  Minestrone, Chilled Summer, 202–3
avocado(s):
  and Grilled Pineapple Salad with Walnut Oil Vinaigrette, 156
  Guacamole, 45–46
  Salad of Arugula, Mango and, 169

Baby Back Ribs, Glazed, 140–41
baking:
  equipment for, 30
  pantry supplies for, 24
Balsamic and Red Onion Vinaigrette, Bibb Lettuce with, 96
Bananas, Vanilla Ice Cream with Caramel Sauce and, 103
bars:
  Brownies, Engagement, 177–78
  Chocolate Date Nut, 54–55
  Lemon-Glazed Pecan and Coconut Squares, 205–6
  Six-Layer, with Chocolate, Pecans and Coconut, Jake and Earl's, 157–58
Basil, Chicken Curry with Coconut, Mangoes and, 100–101
Basmati Rice with Toasted Pistachio Nuts, 102
bean(s):
  Black, Coconut Risotto, 60–61
  Fava, Dip, 48
  fava or lima, in Chilled Summer Minestrone, 202–3

bean(s) (*cont.*)
    Red, Dip, 33
    Three–, Chili with Tons of Garnishes,
      160–61
beef:
    Carbonnade, 106–7
    Flank Steak, Grilled Marinated, with
      Soy, Sherry and Dijon, 166–67
    Steak Tips, Spicy Mustard, 180–81
Belgian dishes:
    Beef Carbonnade, 106–7
    Brussels Sprouts Leaves with Brown
      Butter, 109
berry:
    Puree, Fresh Fruit with, 69
    see also specific berries
Biba (Boston), 48
Bibb Lettuce with Red Onion and Bal-
    samic Vinaigrette, 96
Black Bean Coconut Risotto, 60–61
Blueberry, Nectarine and Strawberry
    Crunch, 195
Bouillabaisse with Rouille, 186–88
bread(s):
    Bruschetta, 32
    Corn, 162
    Garlic, Roasted, 81–82
    Pudding, Chocolate, Drizzled with
      Heavy Cream, 89–90
Brine–Cured Grilled Pork Loin with
    Spanish Tomato Salsa, Ana Sor-
    tun's, 214–16
broccoli rabe:
    Orzo and, 88
    Pasta Alfredo with, 147
Brownies, Engagement, 177–78
Bruschetta, 32
Brussels Sprouts Leaves with Brown
    Butter, 109
Burgers, Lamb, Rosemary Oregano, 66
Butter Cookies, Pecan, 224
    Fresh Figs, Red Grapes and, 129
Butternut Squash, Roasted Granny
    Smith Apples and, with Walnuts
    and Currants, 134

cabbage, in Asian Slaw, 142
Cake (sweet), Carrot, Dain's Grand-
    mother's, 110–11
Cake (savory), Potato, with Garlic and
    Olive Oil, 168
canned foods, 23
Cantaloupe, Cookie Platter, Grapes
    and, 84
Caramel Sauce, Vanilla Ice Cream with
    Bananas and, 103
Caribbean dishes:
    Chicken, Spiced, 58–59
    Coconut Black Bean Risotto, 60–61
carrot(s):
    Cake, Dain's Grandmother's, 110–11
    Slaw, Asian, 142
cashew(s):
    Noodles with Asparagus and Pep-
      pers, 138–39
    Spicy Scallops with, 208–9
Catfish, Spice-Rubbed, 153–54
cheese:
    Cream, Chutney, 35
    Cream, Icing, 110–11
    Feta, Roast Potatoes with, 67
    Feta and Artichoke Dip, 34
    Gorgonzola Dip, 36
    Herb, 41
    Roquefort, Romaine Salad with
      Arugula, Pears and, 189
Cheesecake with Raspberry Sauce,
    170–71
chicken:
    Breasts, Roasted, with Dried Figs,
      Apricots and Prunes, 114–15
    Caribbean Spiced, 58–59
    Curry with Coconut, Basil and Man-
      goes, 100
    Fricassee, 198–99
    Garlic Roasted, with Pan-Roasted
      Vegetables, 86–87
    Moroccan, 50–51
    Saltimbocca with Panfried Sage
      Leaves, 132–33
Chickpea Spread, 43

Chili, Three–Bean, with Tons of Gar-
nishes, 160–61
chocolate:
  Bittersweet, Sauce, Ginger Ice Cream
    with, 143
  Bittersweet, Sauce, Vanilla Ice Cream
    with Raspberries and, 190
  Bread Pudding Drizzled with Heavy
    Cream, 89–90
  Brownies, Engagement, 177–78
  Chip Cookies, 221
  Cocoa Cookies, Crispy, 220
  Date Nut Bars, 54–55
  Glaze, 177–78
  Glaze, Hazelnut Torte with, 148–49
  Mousse Torte, 184
  Six–Layer Bars with Pecans, Coconut
    and, Jake and Earl's, 157–58
Chutney Cream Cheese, 35
cilantro, 58
  Chilled Corn Soup with Tomatoes,
    Red Peppers and, 152
  Paste, Curried Swordfish with, 72–73
Cocoa Cookies, Crispy, 220
coconut:
  Black Bean Risotto, 60–61
  Chicken Curry with Basil, Mangoes
    and, 100–101
  and Pecan Squares, Lemon–Glazed,
    205–6
  Six–Layer Bars with Chocolate,
    Pecans and, Jake and Earl's, 157–58
  Toasted, Key Lime Mousse with,
    63–64
Compote, Strawberry Rhubarb, 76
condiments, in pantry, 23
cookie(s), 219–27
  Chocolate Chip, 221
  Cocoa, Crispy, 220
  Gingersnaps, 222–23
  Hazelnut Shortbread, 225
  Maple, Chewy, 226–27
  Maple, Chewy, and Vanilla Ice
    Cream, 164
  Pecan Butter, 224

Pecan Butter, Fresh Figs, Red Grapes
    and, 129
  Platter, Grapes and Melon, 84
  Platter, Trio of Sorbets and, 136
corn:
  Bread, 162
  Minestrone, Chilled Summer, 202–3
  Oven–Baked, 74
  Soup with Tomatoes, Red Peppers
    and Cilantro, Chilled, 152
cornmeal, in Polenta Triangles, 155
Couscous, Fresh Herb, 52
crackers, 23
cream cheese:
  Chutney, 35
  Icing, 110–11
Crème Brûlée, 218
Crisp, Apple, 200
Crunch, Nectarine, Strawberry and
    Blueberry, 195
crusts, 205
  Graham Cracker or Gingersnap,
    170–71
  Tart, 97–98
cucumber(s):
  Romaine with Tomatoes and, 68
  Salad with Yogurt and Mint, 62
  Tsatsiki, 47
Curd, Lemon, Fresh Raspberry Tart
    with, 97–98
Currants, Roasted Butternut Squash
    and Granny Smith Apples with
    Walnuts and, 134
curry(ied):
  Chicken, with Coconut, Basil and
    Mangoes, 100
  Rub, 72
  Swordfish with Cilantro Paste, 72–73

Date Chocolate Nut Bars, 54–55
desserts:
  Apple Crisp, 200
  Brownies, Engagement, 177–78
  Carrot Cake, Dain's Grandmother's,
    110–11

desserts (*cont.*)
  Cheesecake with Raspberry Sauce, 170–71
  Chocolate Bread Pudding Drizzled with Heavy Cream, 89–90
  Chocolate Date Nut Bars, 54–55
  Chocolate Mousse Torte, 184
  Cookie Platter, Grapes and Melon, 84
  Crème Brûlée, 218
  Figs, Fresh, Red Grapes and Pecan Butter Cookies, 129
  Fruit, Fresh, with Berry Puree, 69
  Ginger Ice Cream with Bittersweet Chocolate Sauce, 143
  Hazelnut Torte with Chocolate Glaze, 148–49
  Key Lime Mousse with Toasted Coconut, 63–64
  Lemon-Glazed Pecan and Coconut Squares, 205–6
  Maple Cookies, Chewy, and Vanilla Ice Cream, 164
  Nectarine, Strawberry and Blueberry Crunch, 195
  Raspberry, Fresh, Tart with Lemon Curd, 97–98
  Rice Pudding, 117–18
  Six-Layer Bars with Chocolate, Pecans and Coconut, Jake and Earl's, 157–58
  Strawberry Rhubarb Compote, 76
  Trio of Sorbets and Cookie Platter, 136
  Vanilla Ice Cream with Bananas and Caramel Sauce, 103
  Vanilla Ice Cream with Bittersweet Chocolate Sauce and Raspberries, 190
  Vanilla Ice Cream with Roasted Peaches and Gingerroot, 211
  see also cookie(s)
Dijon, Soy and Sherry Marinade, 166–67
dips, 33–48
  Artichoke and Feta, 34
  Caramelized Onion, 39–40
  Chutney Cream Cheese, 35
  Fava Bean, 48
  Gorgonzola, 36
  Guacamole, 45–46
  Herb Cheese, 41
  Red Bean, 33
  Roasted Red Pepper, with Walnuts and Pomegranate Molasses, 37–38
  Salsa, Basic, 44
  Sesame, Spicy, 42
  Tsatsiki, 47

East Coast Grill (Boston), 157
egg(s):
  Avgolemono Soup (Greek egg lemon soup), 124
  raw, safety concerns and, 184
eggplant(s):
  and Lamb Moussaka, 125–27
  Ratatouille, Roasted, 193
Endive, Salad of Arugula, Radicchio and, 83
English, Todd, 67
equipment, 27–30
  for baking, 30
  gadgets, 28–29
  knives, 29–30
  pots and pans, 29

fava bean(s):
  Dip, 48
  Minestrone, Chilled Summer, 202–203
Fennel Shrimp, Pan-Broiled, Saffron Risotto with, 92–94
feta cheese:
  and Artichoke Dip, 34
  Roast Potatoes with, 67
figs:
  Dried, Roasted Chicken Breasts with Apricots, Prunes and, 114–15
  Fresh, Red Grapes and Pecan Butter Cookies, 129
  Fresh Fruit with Berry Puree, 69

fish:
  Bouillabaisse with Rouille, 186–88
  Catfish, Spice–Rubbed, 153–54
  Salmon Steaks, Grilled, with Citrus
    and Thyme, 174
  Swordfish, Curried, with Cilantro
    Paste, 72–73
  Tuna au Poivre, 192
Fizzy Lizzy, 37
Flank Steak, Grilled Marinated, with
  Soy, Sherry and Dijon, 166–67
freezer items, 25
French dishes:
  Bouillabaisse with Rouille, 186–88
  Crème Brûlée, 218
  Potatoes, New, Roasted, 194
  Ratatouille, Roasted, 193
  Tuna au Poivre, 192
Fricassee, Chicken, 198–99
fruit(s):
  Fresh, with Berry Puree, 69
  in pantry, 24–25
  see also specific fruits
Full Moon (Boston), 157

gadgets, 28–29
garlic:
  Bread, Roasted, 81–82
  Potato Cake with Olive Oil and,
    168
ginger (root):
  Ice Cream with Bittersweet Choco-
    late Sauce, 143
  Vanilla Ice Cream with Roasted
    Peaches and, 211
Gingersnap(s), 222–23
  Crust, 170–71
glazes:
  Asian, for ribs, 140
  Chocolate, 148, 177–78
  Lemon, 205–6
Gorgonzola Dip, 36
Graham Cracker Crust, 170–71
grapes:
  Cookie Platter, Melon and, 84

Red, Fresh Figs and Pecan Butter
  Cookies, 129
Greek dishes:
  Avgolemono Soup, 124
  Eggplant and Lamb Moussaka,
    125–27
  Lamb Burgers, Rosemary Oregano,
    66
  Potatoes, Roast, with Feta Cheese, 67
  Romaine with Cucumbers and
    Tomatoes, 68
  Tsatsiki, 47
Greens, Seared, 183
green salads:
  Arugula, Endive and Radicchio, 83
  Bibb Lettuce with Red Onion and
    Balsamic Vinaigrette, 96
  with Creamy Orange Dressing, 163
  Mixed, with Pistachio-Lemon Dress-
    ing, 128
  Mixed, with Red Onions and Toasted
    Pine Nuts, 116
  Romaine, with Anchovy Dressing, 135
grilled dishes:
  Asparagus, 217
  Catfish, Spice–Rubbed, 153–54
  Flank Steak Marinated with Soy,
    Sherry and Dijon, 166–67
  Pork Loin, Brine–Cured, with Span-
    ish Tomato Salsa, Ana Sortun's,
    214–16
  Salmon Steaks with Citrus and
    Thyme, 174
  Shrimp Skewers, 204
Guacamole, 45–46

hazelnut:
  Shortbread, 225
  Torte with Chocolate Glaze, 148–49
Heatter, Maida, 184
Henckels, 29
herb(s):
  Cheese, 41
  dried, 21
  Fresh, Couscous, 52

ice cream:
    Ginger, with Bittersweet Chocolate
      Sauce, 143
    Vanilla, Chewy Maple Cookies and,
      164
    Vanilla, with Bananas and Caramel
      Sauce, 103
    Vanilla, with Bittersweet Chocolate
      Sauce and Raspberries, 190
    Vanilla, with Roasted Peaches and
      Gingerroot, 211
Icing, Cream Cheese, 110–11
Indian dishes:
    Basmati Rice with Toasted Pistachio
      Nuts, 102
    Chicken Curry with Coconut, Basil
      and Mangoes, 100
Italian dishes:
    Bruschetta, 32
    Chicken Saltimbocca with Panfried
      Sage Leaves, 132–33
    Coconut Black Bean Risotto, 60–61
    Garlic Bread, Roasted, 81
    Lasagna, Classic, 78–80
    Minestrone, Chilled Summer, 202–3
    Pasta Alfredo with Broccoli Rabe,
      147
    Polenta Triangles, 155
    Prosciutto–Wrapped Mango Slices,
      146
    Shrimp, Pan–Broiled Fennel, Saffron
      Risotto with, 92–94
    Wild Mushroom Risotto with Radic-
      chio Salad, 121–22

Jake and Earl's Dixie BBQ (Boston),
    157
Joy of Cooking, 170

Kaiser La Forme, 30
Key Lime Mousse with Toasted Co-
    conut, 63–64
kiwis, in Fresh Fruit with Berry Puree,
    69
knives, 29–30

lamb:
    Burgers, Rosemary Oregano, 66
    and Eggplant Moussaka, 125–27
Lasagna, Classic, 78–80
Leek Mashed Potatoes, 176
lemon:
    Avgolemono Soup (Greek egg lemon
      soup), 124
    Curd, Fresh Raspberry Tart with,
      97–98
    –Glazed Pecan and Coconut Squares,
      205–6
    Pistachio Dressing, Mixed Greens
      with, 128
lima beans, in Chilled Summer Mine-
    strone, 202–3
lime:
    juice, key vs. fresh, 63
    Key, Mousse with Toasted Coconut,
      63–64

main dishes:
    Baby Back Ribs, Glazed, 140–41
    Beef Carbonnade, 106–7
    Bouillabaisse with Rouille, 186–88
    Catfish, Spice–Rubbed, 153–54
    Chicken, Caribbean Spiced, 58–59
    Chicken, Garlic Roasted, with Pan-
      Roasted Vegetables, 86–87
    Chicken, Moroccan, 50–51
    Chicken Breasts, Roasted, with Dried
      Figs, Apricots and, Prunes, 114–15
    Chicken Curry with Coconut, Basil
      and Mangoes, 100
    Chicken Fricassee, 198–99
    Chicken Saltimbocca with Panfried
      Sage Leaves, 132–33
    Eggplant and Lamb Moussaka,
      125–27
    Flank Steak, Grilled Marinated, with
      Soy, Sherry and Dijon, 166–67
    Lamb Burgers, Rosemary Oregano, 66
    Lasagna, Classic, 78–80
    Pasta Alfredo with Broccoli Rabe,
      147

Pork Loin, Brine-Cured Grilled, with Spanish Tomato Salsa, Ana Sortun's, 214–16
Salmon Steaks, Grilled, with Citrus and Thyme, 174
Scallops with Cashews, Spicy, 208–9
Shrimp, Pan-Broiled Fennel, Saffron Risotto with, 92–94
Shrimp Skewers, Grilled, 204
Steak Tips, Spicy Mustard, 180–81
Swordfish, Curried, with Cilantro Paste, 72–73
Three-Bean Chili with Tons of Garnishes, 160–61
Tuna au Poivre, 192
Wild Mushroom Risotto with Radicchio Salad, 121–22
mango(es):
    Chicken Curry with Coconut, Basil and, 100–101
    Salad of Arugula, Avocado and, 169
    Slices, Prosciutto-Wrapped, 146
Maple Cookies, Chewy, 226–27
    and Vanilla Ice Cream, 164
marinades:
    for chicken, 114
    for steak, 166–67
mashed:
    Potatoes, Leek, 176
    Potatoes, Parsnip, 108
    Sweet Potatoes, 182
Melon, Cookie Platter, Grapes and, 84
Mexican dishes:
    Guacamole, 45–46
    Salsa, Basic, 44
    Three-Bean Chili with Tons of Garnishes, 160–61
Minestrone, Chilled Summer, 202–3
Mint, Cucumber Salad with Yogurt and, 62
mixed green(s):
    with Pistachio-Lemon Dressing, 128
    Salad with Red Onions and Toasted Pine Nuts, 116

Moroccan dishes:
    Chicken, 50–51
    Couscous, Fresh Herb, 52
Moussaka, Eggplant and Lamb, 125–127
mousse:
    Chocolate, Torte, 184
    Key Lime, with Toasted Coconut, 63–64
    Mushroom, Wild, Risotto with Radicchio Salad, 121–22
mussels, in Bouillabaisse with Rouille, 186–88
mustard:
    Dijon, Soy and Sherry Marinade, 166–67
    Steak Tips, Spicy, 180–81

Nectarine, Strawberry and Blueberry Crunch, 195
Noodles, Cashew, with Asparagus and Peppers, 138–39
nut(s):
    Chocolate Date Bars, 54–55
    toasting, 102
    see also specific nuts

oils, in pantry, 23
onion(s):
    Caramelized, Dip, 39–40
    Red, and Balsamic Vinaigrette, Bibb Lettuce with, 96
    Red, and Blood Orange Salad, 53
    Red, Mixed Green Salad with Toasted Pine Nuts and, 116
orange(s):
    Blood, and Red Onion Salad, 53
    blood, in Fresh Fruit with Berry Puree, 69
    Dressing, Creamy, Green Salad with, 163
    Segments, Watercress Salad with, 210
Oregano Rosemary Lamb Burgers, 66
Orzo and Broccoli Rabe, 88

pans, 29
pantry, 21–25
    baking supplies in, 24
    canned foods in, 23
    condiments, oils and vinegars in, 23
    dried herbs and spices in, 21–22
    freezer items in, 25
    fruits and vegetables in, 24–25
    pasta, rice and crackers in, 23
    refrigerator items in, 24
Parsnip Mashed Potatoes, 108
pasta:
    Alfredo with Broccoli Rabe, 147
    Cashew Noodles with Asparagus
        and Peppers, 138–39
    Lasagna, Classic, 78–80
    Orzo and Broccoli Rabe, 88
    in pantry, 23
Peaches, Roasted, Vanilla Ice Cream
        with Gingerroot and, 211
Pears, Romaine Salad with Arugula,
        Roquefort Cheese and, 189
peas, in Chilled Summer Minestrone,
        202–3
pecan(s):
    Butter Cookies, 224
    Butter Cookies, Fresh Figs, Red
        Grapes and, 129
    and Coconut Squares, Lemon-
        Glazed, 205–6
    Six-Layer Bars with Chocolate, Co-
        conut and, Jake and Earl's, 157–58
Penzey's Spices, 21, 180
pepper(s):
    Cashew Noodles with Asparagus
        and, 138–39
    Red, Chilled Corn Soup with Toma-
        toes, Cilantro and, 152
    Roasted Red, Dip with Walnuts and
        Pomegranate Molasses, 37–38
pepper (black), in Tuna au Poivre, 192
Pineapple, Grilled, and Avocado Salad
        with Walnut Oil Vinaigrette, 156
Pine Nuts, Toasted, Mixed Green Salad
        ·with Red Onions and, 116

pistachio nut(s):
    Lemon Dressing, Mixed Greens with,
        128
    Toasted, Basmati Rice with, 102
Polenta Triangles, 155
pomegranate molasses:
    Fizzy Lizzy, 37
    Roasted Red Pepper Dip with Wal-
        nuts and, 37–38
pork:
    Baby Back Ribs, Glazed, 140–41
    Loin, Brine–Cured Grilled, with
        Spanish Tomato Salsa, Ana Sor-
        tun's, 214–16
potato(es):
    Cake with Garlic and Olive Oil, 168
    Leek Mashed, 176
    New, Roasted, 194
    Parsnip Mashed, 108
    Roast, with Feta Cheese, 67
    see also sweet potato(es)
pots, 29
Prosciutto-Wrapped Mango Slices, 146
Provençal dishes:
    Bouillabaisse with Rouille, 186–88
    Potatoes, New, Roasted, 194
    Ratatouille, Roasted, 193
    Tuna au Poivre, 192
Prunes, Roasted Chicken Breasts with
        Dried Figs, Apricots and, 114–15
puddings:
    Chocolate Bread, Drizzled with
        Heavy Cream, 89–90
    Rice, 117–18

radicchio:
    Salad, Wild Mushroom Risotto with,
        121–22
    Salad of Arugula, Endive and, 83
raspberry(ies):
    Fresh, Tart with Lemon Curd, 97–98
    Puree, Fresh Fruit with, 69
    Sauce, Cheesecake with, 170–71
    Vanilla Ice Cream with Bittersweet
        Chocolate Sauce and, 190

Ratatouille, Roasted, 193
Red Bean Dip, 33
refrigerator items, in pantry, 24
Regis, Susan, 48, 131
Rhubarb Strawberry Compote, 76
Ribs, Baby Back, Glazed, 140–41
rice:
    Basmati, with Toasted Pistachio Nuts,
        102
    in pantry, 23
    Pudding, 117–18
risotto:
    Coconut Black Bean, 60–61
    Saffron, with Pan-Broiled Fennel
        Shrimp, 92–94
    Wild Mushroom, with Radicchio
        Salad, 121–22
romaine:
    with Cucumbers and Tomatoes, 68
    Salad with Anchovy Dressing, 135
    Salad with Arugula, Roquefort
        Cheese and Pears, 189
Roquefort Cheese, Romaine Salad with
    Arugula, Pears and, 189
Rosemary Oregano Lamb Burgers, 66
Rouille, Bouillabaisse with, 186–88
rubs:
    Curry, 72
    Spice, 153

Sabatier, 29
Saffron Risotto with Pan-Broiled Fen-
    nel Shrimp, 92–94
Sage Leaves, Panfried, Chicken Saltim-
    bocca with, 132–33
salad dressings, 169
    Anchovy, 135
    Asian, 142
    Cashew, 138–39
    Greek, 68
    Orange, Creamy, 163
    Pistachio-Lemon, 128
    Red Onion and Balsamic Vinaigrette,
        96
    Walnut Oil Vinaigrette, 156

salads:
    of Arugula, Avocado and Mango,
        169
    of Arugula, Endive and Radicchio, 83
    Asparagus, Fresh, 120
    Bibb Lettuce with Red Onion and
        Balsamic Vinaigrette, 96
    Cashew Noodles with Asparagus
        and Peppers, 138–39
    Cucumber, with Yogurt and Mint, 62
    Green, with Creamy Orange Dress-
        ing, 163
    Mixed Green, with Red Onions and
        Toasted Pine Nuts, 116
    Mixed Greens with Pistachio-Lemon
        Dressing, 128
    Pineapple, Grilled, and Avocado,
        with Walnut Oil Vinaigrette, 156
    Radicchio, Wild Mushroom Risotto
        with, 121–22
    Red Onion and Blood Orange, 53
    Romaine, with Anchovy Dressing,
        135
    Romaine, with Arugula, Roquefort
        Cheese and Pears, 189
    Romaine with Cucumbers and
        Tomatoes, 68
    Slaw, Asian, 142
    Watercress, with Orange Segments,
        210
Salmon Steaks, Grilled, with Citrus and
    Thyme, 174
salsas:
    Basic, 44
    Tomato, Spanish, 214–15
Saltimbocca, Chicken, with Panfried
    Sage Leaves, 132–33
Sapoznik, Carol and Maury, 131
sauces:
    Chocolate, Bittersweet, 190
    Raspberry, 171
scallops:
    Bouillabaisse with Rouille, 186–88
    with Cashews, Spicy, 208–9
Schlesinger, Chris, 157

Sesame Dip, Spicy, 42
shellfish:
    Bouillabaisse with Rouille, 186–88
    Scallops with Cashews, Spicy, 208–9
    Shrimp, Pan-Broiled Fennel, Saffron
        Risotto with, 92–94
    Shrimp Skewers, Grilled, 204
Sherry, Soy and Dijon Marinade, 166–67
Shire, Lydia, 48
Shortbread, Hazelnut, 225
shrimp:
    Bouillabaisse with Rouille, 186–88
    Pan-Broiled Fennel, Saffron Risotto
        with, 92–94
    Skewers, Grilled, 204
side dishes:
    Asparagus, Fresh, Salad, 120
    Asparagus, Grilled, 217
    Basmati Rice with Toasted Pistachio
        Nuts, 102
    Bibb Lettuce with Red Onion and
        Balsamic Vinaigrette, 96
    Brussels Sprouts Leaves with Brown
        Butter, 109
    Butternut Squash and Granny Smith
        Apples, Roasted, with Walnuts and
        Currants, 134
    Cashew Noodles with Asparagus
        and Peppers, 138–39
    Coconut Black Bean Risotto, 60–61
    Corn, Oven-Baked, 74
    Corn Bread, 162
    Couscous, Fresh Herb, 52
    Cucumber Salad with Yogurt and
        Mint, 62
    Garlic Bread, Roasted, 81–82
    Greens, Seared, 183
    Green Salad with Creamy Orange
        Dressing, 163
    Leek Mashed Potatoes, 176
    Mixed Green Salad with Red Onions
        and Toasted Pine Nuts, 116
    Mixed Greens with Pistachio-Lemon
        Dressing, 128
    Orzo and Broccoli Rabe, 88
    Parsnip Mashed Potatoes, 108

Pineapple, Grilled, and Avocado
        Salad with Walnut Oil Vinaigrette,
        156
    Polenta Triangles, 155
    Potato Cake with Garlic and Olive
        Oil, 168
    Potatoes, New, Roasted, 194
    Potatoes, Roast, with Feta Cheese, 67
    Ratatouille, Roasted, 193
    Romaine Salad with Anchovy Dress-
        ing, 135
    Romaine Salad with Arugula,
        Roquefort Cheese and Pears, 189
    Romaine with Cucumbers and
        Tomatoes, 68
    Salad of Arugula, Avocado and
        Mango, 169
    Salad of Arugula, Endive and Radic-
        chio, 83
    Slaw, Asian, 142
    Spinach, Pan-Steamed, 175
    Sweet Potatoes, Mashed, 182
    Tomatoes, Cherry, Sautéed, 75
    Tomato Salsa, Spanish, 214–15
    Watercress Salad with Orange Seg-
        ments, 210
    Zucchini, Pan-Broiled, 95
Six-Layer Bars with Chocolate, Pecans
        and Coconut, Jake and Earl's,
        157–58
Slaw, Asian, 142
Sorbets, Trio of, and Cookie Platter, 136
Sortun, Ana, 213, 214
soups:
    Avgolemono, 124
    Corn, with Tomatoes, Red Peppers
        and Cilantro, Chilled, 152
    Minestrone, Chilled Summer, 202–3
Soy, Sherry and Dijon Marinade,
        166–67
Spanish Tomato Salsa, Brine-Cured
        Grilled Pork Loin with, Ana Sor-
        tun's, 214–16
spice(d)(s):
    Caribbean Chicken, 58–59
    in pantry, 21

Rub, 153
–Rubbed Catfish, 153–54
spicy:
   Mustard Steak Tips, 180–81
   Scallops with Cashews, 208–9
   Sesame Dip, 42
Spinach, Pan-Steamed, 175
spreads:
   Chickpea, 43
   see also dips
squash:
   Butternut, Roasted Granny Smith
      Apples and, with Walnuts and
      Currants, 134
   see also zucchini
steak:
   Flank, Grilled Marinated, with Soy,
      Sherry and Dijon, 166–67
   Tips, Spicy Mustard, 180–81
stews:
   Beef Carbonnade, 106–7
   Bouillabaisse with Rouille, 186–88
   Chicken Fricassee, 198–99
strawberry:
   Nectarine and Blueberry Crunch, 195
   Rhubarb Compote, 76
Stuart, Cynthia, 192
sweet potato(es):
   Cake with Garlic and Olive Oil, 168
   Mashed, 182
Swordfish, Curried, with Cilantro
   Paste, 72–73

Tarts, Fresh Raspberry, with Lemon
   Curd, 97–98
Three-Bean Chili with Tons of Gar-
   nishes, 160–61
tomato(es):
   Cherry, Sautéed, 75
   Chilled Corn Soup with Red Pep-
      pers, Cilantro and, 152
   Romaine with Cucumbers and, 68
   Salsa, Basic, 44
   Salsa, Spanish, 214–15
tortes:
   Chocolate Mousse, 184

Hazelnut, with Chocolate Glaze,
   148–49
Tsatsiki, 47
Tuna au Poivre, 192

vanilla ice cream:
   with Bananas and Caramel Sauce,
      103
   with Bittersweet Chocolate Sauce
      and Raspberries, 190
   Chewy Maple Cookies and, 164
   with Roasted Peaches and Ginger-
      root, 211
vegetables:
   Pan-Roasted, Garlic Roasted Chicken
      with, 86–87
   in pantry, 24–25
   see also specific vegetables
vinaigrettes:
   Red Onion and Balsamic, 96
   Walnut Oil, 156
vinegars, 23

Walnut Oil Vinaigrette, 156
walnuts:
   Roasted Butternut Squash and
      Granny Smith Apples with Cur-
      rants and, 134
   Roasted Red Pepper Dip with
      Pomegranate Molasses and, 37–38
watercress:
   Grilled Pineapple and Avocado
      Salad with Walnut Oil Vinaigrette,
      156
   Salad with Orange Segments, 210
Wheaton, Cary, 157
Wusthof/Dreizack, 29

yogurt:
   Cucumber Salad with Mint and,
      62
   Tsatsiki, 47

zucchini:
   Pan-Broiled, 95
   Ratatouille, Roasted, 193